INSIGHTS
INTO
ENGLISH STRUCTURE

INSIGHTS
INTO
ENGLISH STRUCTURE:
A Programmed Course

RUSSELL N. CAMPBELL
University of California, Los Angeles

JUDITH W. LINDFORS
University of California, Los Angeles

This was a research project financed jointly
by the University of California at Los Angeles
and the Peace Corps.

PRENTICE-HALL INC., Englewood Cliffs, New Jersey

13-467571-1

Printed in the United States of America

Current Printing (last number):

10   9

PRENTICE-HALL INTERNATIONAL, INC., *London*
PRENTICE-HALL OF AUSTRALIA, PTY. LTD., *Sydney*
PRENTICE-HALL OF CANADA, LTD., *Toronto*
PRENTICE-HALL OF INDIA PRIVATE LIMITED, *New Delhi*
PRENTICE-HALL OF JAPAN, INC., *Tokyo*

PREFACE

Beginning in the third or fourth grade and continuing through elementary school, junior high, and high school, and into at least the second year of college, all students take courses in English. Even with this in mind, however, it is difficult to disagree with H. A. Gleason's claim:

> Adult Americans are badly informed about language and endemically prone to naive reasoning on any linguistic question. Moreover, they have no better insight into their own English tongue than into language in general, and this is, perhaps, the most serious failure of liberal humanistic objectives in American education.
>
> (*Harvard Educational Review* 34.267, 1964)

This three-part, programmed text is not going to remedy that situation in some magical fashion. However, it does provide interested readers—whether they be high school students, university students, teachers, or laymen—with an opportunity to gain some insight into the structure of the English language. This book explains, to some degree, the remarkable facility to produce and understand an infinite number of English utterances.

PART ONE of the text teaches the reader to identify and describe in analytical terms the consonants and vowels he uses to produce typically English utterances (Phonology).

PART TWO develops an understanding of the regularity of the internal structure of English words (Morphology).

PART THREE initiates the reader to the internal structure of English sentences, as well as to the systematic relationships of sentences to each other (Syntax).

Since the text is self-instructional, it may be used as a complement or a supplement to other texts used in English language or elementary linguistics courses. It can also be used as the main text in a number of short-term introductory courses in the structure of English.

The authors are extremely grateful to the large number of Peace Corps Volunteers, students, teachers, and colleagues who have participated either as consumers or critics in the development of this book. The preparation and reproduction of the numerous preliminary versions of the material were made possible by a joint Peace Corps-University of California, Los Angeles grant, for which we are very appreciative. We wish also to recognize with gratitude the excellent work of Miss Joanne March who patiently typed and retyped many experimental editions of the program as well as the final manuscript.

R.N.C.
J.W.L.

CONTENTS

INSIGHTS
INTO
ENGLISH STRUCTURE

Suppose you wanted to explain to somebody, say to a speaker of Spanish or Chinese (or just to yourself), what you do to differentiate the pronunciations of *thanks* and *tanks* so that other speakers of English know which word you are saying. What do you tell him? Or perhaps you have noticed that the letters *th* are pronounced differently in the words *Thomas*, *thank*, and *than*. (Pronounce each word out loud to hear the difference.) Just what is the relation between the letters we use to represent English words and the sounds we use to form those words? Is the number of letters in our alphabet equal to the number of sounds we use? Is the same sound always spelled the same way? (Say these words out loud, concentrating on the initial sound in each: *ship*, *sugar*, *Chicago*.)

Part One of this course will lead you to answers to these and other questions about the sounds of English. The material is programmed for self-instruction. This means that you may work through it at your own pace and at times convenient for you. The instructions are simple: Cover the answers on the left-hand side of the page; read each numbered frame; and write the answer in the space provided. (Often it will help if you read the questions out loud.) Then check your answer with the one given. If your answer is correct, continue to the next frame. If your answer is incorrect: (1) *circle* the correct answer, (2) cross out your answer, (3) reread the frame, and (4) write the correct answer.

THE SOUNDS OF ENGLISH

SECTION 1

In Section 1 you will study nine English sounds. At the end of this lesson you will be able to:

a) identify these sounds in English words;
b) recognize and write a symbol for each sound;
c) label diagrams showing the parts of the mouth that are important in the production of these sounds;
d) describe how these sounds are made;
e) label three categories to which these nine sounds belong;
f) list these sounds in three appropriate categories.

---

the first

1. The three words *pay*, *bay*, and *may* sound very much alike. However, as speakers of English we distinguish one from the other quite easily. What part of each word separates it from the other two? ....
....

p, b, and m

2. What we are saying is that *pay*, *bay*, and *may* are alike except for the first sound in each word. The three different sounds are represented in these words by the letters ...., ..., and ....

yes

The lips are together, touching, closed, etc.

3. Now say *bay*, *pay*, and *may*. Notice the position of your lips as you begin the first sound in each word. (Use a mirror if you like.) Is the position of your lips the same for all three (*b, p, m*)? .... In your own words, describe the position of your lips.
....
....

yes

4. Now let's put *b*, *p*, and *m* at the end of some words. Do your lips come together when you make *b, p*, and *m* sounds in these words: *rib, rip, rim*? ....

5. The sounds *b, p, m* are always produced by bringing the lips together. These sounds are called **bilabial**

3

sounds or simply **bilabials**. Look at the following facial diagrams:

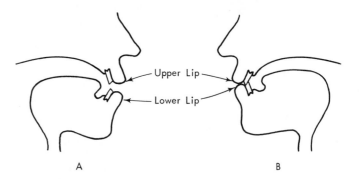

Which diagram shows the lips in position to produce a bilabial? ....

B

6. The first sounds of *bay*, *pay*, and *may* are the .... sounds of English. They are the three sounds that are made by ....

bilabial
bringing the lips together,
closing the lips, etc.

7. Using each of the bilabials once in each column, complete these words:

bat	mob	bad
pat	mop	pad
mat	mom	mad

............at   mo............   ....ad
............at   mo............   ....ad
............at   mo............   ....ad

8. Which of the following words contain bilabial sounds?

phone   phase   receipt
doubt   sphere   debt

none of them

9. During the production of a bilabial the lips are brought completely together. Do your lips completely close as you say *phone*, *doubt*, *phase*, *sphere*, *receipt*, *debt*?

....

no

10. *Phone*, *phase*, *sphere*, and *receipt* contain the letter *p*. *Doubt* and *debt* contain the letter *b*. But none of these words contains the .... sound /b/ or /p/. We will use diagonal lines (/   /) to show that we are representing sounds rather than letters.

bilabial

4

sounds

/b/ and /p/ represent ...., they do not represent letters.

11. As speakers of English we differentiate words like *pay* and *bay* by choosing either /p/ or /b/ just as we differentiate *may* from both *pay* and *bay* by choosing /m/. A convenient term to use for sounds that separate one word from another is **phoneme**. Thus /p/, /b/, and /m/ are three of the phonemes of English. Is the first sound

yes   It separates *say* from other words (e.g., *bay*, *pay*, and *may*).

in *say* (/s/) also a phoneme? .... Explain. ....

....

/g/   /t/

12. What two phonemes are demonstrated in the contrasting pair *bag* and *bat*? /   / and /   /.

13. *Slid* and *slip* demonstrate that /d/ and /p/ are two

phonemes

different ....

/f/
/v/

14. *Fan* is one word and *van* is a different word. /   / and /   / are phonemes.

they separate or distinguish words; they separate the word *Tim* from *tin*

15. We know that /m/ (as in *Tim*) and /n/ (as in *tin*) are separate phonemes because ....

....

no   The lips are not brought together, do not close, etc.

16. Say these words: *tip*, *dip*, *nip*. Are the initial phonemes of these three words (i.e., /t/, /d/, /n/) bilabials? .... Explain. ....

....

It is immediately behind (but not touching) the upper teeth.

17. Start to say *dip* but don't say it. What is the position of the tip of your tongue?...

....

....

18. During the production of /d/ as in *dip*, the tip of the tongue makes contact with the gum ridge or **alveolar ridge** behind the upper teeth as illustrated in the diagram.

5

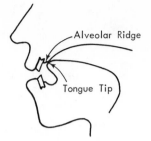

Alveolar Ridge

Tongue Tip

Sounds produced with the tongue tip touching the alveolar ridge are called **alveolar sounds** (or simply **alveolars**). /d/ is a(n) ....

alveolar

19. Start to say *tip* but don't say it. What is the position of the tip of the tongue during the production of /t/?

The same as for /d/; i.e., it touches the alveolar ridge.

....

....

alveolar
the tip of the tongue touches the alveolar ridge when /d/ is pronounced

20. Like /t/, /d/ is a(n) .... sound because ....
....

It is an alveolar, or the tongue tip touches the alveolar ridge when /n/ is pronounced.

21. Start to say *nip* but don't say it. In what way is /n/ like /t/ and /d/? ....
....
....

yes   (/n/)

22. Is the first sound in *know* an alveolar? ....

/t/   alveolar

23. /n/, /d/, and /   / are all .... sounds.

/p/ /b/ /m/
(as in *pay*, *bay*, *may*)
/t/ /d/ /n/
(as in *tip*, *dip*, *nip*)

24. We have now identified three bilabial phonemes (/   /, /   /, and /   /), and three alveolar phonemes (/   /, /   /, and /   /).

25. When a speech sound is produced, a stream of air expelled from the lungs passes through the throat and is finally released through the mouth or nose. The terms bilabial and alveolar, which we have used to describe /p, b, m/ and /t, d, n/, identify places or points where the stream of air is modified in the oral cavity.

the lips

the alveolar ridge

points
articulation

the air stream is modified
at the alveolar ridge

the air stream is modified

c

back

the back part

back
velum

These places are called **points of articulation.** Where is the air stream modified during the production of a bilabial? .... Where is the air stream modified during the production of an alveolar?
....

26. Bilabial and alveolar name two ....
    of ....

27. We say that the point of articulation for /t/, /d/, and /n/ is alveolar since ....
    ....

28. A point of articulation is the place in the mouth where
    ....
    during the production of a particular sound.

29. /k/ is the first sound of the word *kite*. However, /k/ is not always spelled with the letter *k*. How is /k/ spelled in the word car? ....

30. The point of articulation for /k/ is different from the two points we have studied so far. Pronounce the bilabial /p/ and the alveolar /t/ and then /k/ several times in succession, /p-t-k, p-t-k, p-t-k, p-t-k/. The air stream is modified farther .... (*front* or *back*) in the mouth for /k/ than for /p/ or /t/.

31. When we produce the sound /k/, contact is made between the tongue and the soft palate or **velum**. When we make alveolar sounds, it is the tip of the tongue that touches the alveolar ridge. Produce the first sound of *kite*. What part of the tongue touches the velum when we produce /k/? ....
    ....

32. /k/ is called a **velar** sound, that is, a sound made by bringing the .... of the tongue in contact with the ...., or soft palate.

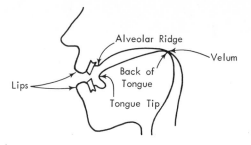

point
articulation

33. Velar names a .... of
...., that is, a point in
the mouth where the air stream from the lungs is
modified.

34. Label this diagram as indicated. If you have difficulty,
look at the diagrams in Frames 5, 18, and 32 again.

1) lips
2) tongue tip
3) alveolar ridge
4) velum
5) back of tongue

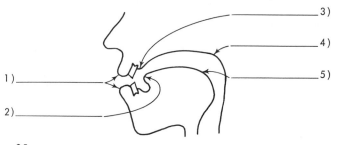

35.

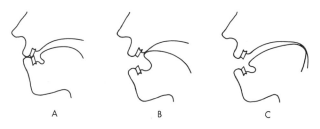

These diagrams show three points of articulation. You
know that Diagram A shows the production of a

are together (closed)   bilabial because the lips ....
                             You know that Diagram B shows the production of
alveolar   a(n) .... sound because the tip of
is touching (in contact   the tongue..
with) the alveolar ridge
                             ....
                             And you know that Diagram C shows the production
is touching (in contact   of a velar sound because the back of the tongue ....
with) the velum
                             ....

36. A point of articulation is the place in the mouth
the air stream is modified   where.. .

8

velar
It is also a velar sound.

back
velum (soft palate)

a), c), d)
[The g in b), e), and f) will
be discussed later.]

/k/   /g/

ng

yes

/ŋ/

/k/   /g/
/ŋ/

a) /n/   f) /b/
b) /k/   g) /k/
c) /n/   h) /m/
d) /t/   i) /p/
e) /d/   j) /g/

37. The final phoneme of *bag* is /g/. Say *back* and *bag*.
/k/ is a .... sound. What kind of
sound is /g/? ....

38. Like /k/, /g/ is produced by contact of the ....
of the tongue with the ....

39. /g/ is a symbol to represent one English sound, namely
the last sound in *bag* or the first sound in *go*. The letter
g may be used in our spelling system to represent
several sounds. Which of the following words contain
the sound /g/?

    a) gun   c) girl   e) badge
    b) gin   d) pig   f) gem

40. There is one more velar sound in English in addition
to /   / and /   /. It is the last sound in the word
bang. You will remember that the last sound of *back*,
/k/, was spelled with the two letters *ck*. The last sound
of the word *bang* is spelled with the two letters ....

41. The symbol for the last sound of *bang* is /ŋ/. Notice
that it is one phoneme. It is **not** /n/ (as in *sin*) + /g/ (as
in *bag*). Now say *back*, *bag*, and *bang*. We have identified /k/ and /g/ as velars. Is /ŋ/ also a velar? ....

42. The final sound in the word *king* is /   /.

43. The three velars of English are /   /, /   /, and
/   /.

44. Write the symbol for the first sound in each of the
following words. Pronounce each word before you
answer.

    EXAMPLE: boy /b/

    a) knife   / /   f) blight / /
    b) creep   / /   g) come / /
    c) pneumonia / /   h) music / /
    d) trust   / /   i) pure / /
    e) driven   / /   j) gleam / /

45. Write the symbol for the final sound in each of the following words. Pronounce each word before you answer.

EXAMPLE: bad   /d/

a) /n/   g) /m/
b) /n/   h) /ŋ/
c) /p/   i) /t/
d) /m/   j) /ŋ/
e) /d/   k) /k/
f) /g/   l) /b/

a) tune   /   /   g) comb   /   /
b) son   /   /   h) rung   /   /
c) hump   /   /   i) stopped /   /
d) came   /   /   j) walking /   /
e) stabbed /   /   k) clock   /   /
f) log   /   /   l) tub   /   /

(Did you answer /d/ for word i)? If you did, you are still confusing letters with sounds. The last **letter** of *stopped* is *d*; the last **sound** of *stopped* is not /d/.)

46. In Frame 45, words c), d), g), and l) end with

bilabial

alveolar

velar

.... sounds; a), b), e), and i) end with .... sounds; f), h), j), and k) end with .... sounds.

47. The sounds we have studied in this section include:

/p/   /b/   /m/
/t/   /d/   /n/
/k/   /g/   /ŋ/

the three bilabials /   /, /   /, /   /;
the three alveolars /   /, /   /, /   /;
the three velars /   /, /   /, /   /.

SUMMARY OF FRAMES 1–47

The speech sounds we have been studying require a stream of air coming up from the lungs to be released eventually through the nose or mouth. This air stream may be interrupted and modified at different points in the mouth. Points at which the air stream is interrupted are called points of articulation. We have now studied nine of the contrastive sounds (phonemes) of English in the following groups: (1) the bilabials (/p, b, m/) whose point of articulation is the lips, (2) the alveolars (/t, d, n/) whose point of articulation is the alveolar ridge, and (3) the velars (/k, g, ŋ/) whose point of articulation is the velum (soft palate).

The air stream is interrupted in different ways for bilabials, alveolars, and velars. During the production of bilabials, the interruption is the closing of the lips. During the production of alveolars, it is the contact of the tip of the tongue with the alveolar ridge (gum ridge). And for the articulation of velars, the interruption is the contact of the back of the tongue with the velum.

In Section 2 you will study six new sounds and several additional features of the articulation of sounds. By the end of this section you will be able to:

a) identify six more English phonemes and write the phonemic symbol for each;

b) describe six more English phonemes in terms of voicing, the point of articulation, and the manner of articulation;

c) identify facial diagrams showing the production of each of fifteen English phonemes;

d) label and describe two more points of articulation, three methods of air release, and two states of vocal cord activity;

e) list fifteen English phonemes in appropriate categories according to the activity of the vocal cords, points of articulation, and manner of articulation.

SECTION 2

---

48. During the production of speech sounds, the air stream is directed either through the nose or through the mouth. When you say /b/ and /p/, the air is released through the .... But when you say /m/, air is released through the ....

mouth
nose

49. Sounds made by releasing air through the mouth are called **oral sounds**. Those made by the passage of air through the nose are called **nasal sounds** (or simply **nasals**). If you fill the blanks in ....ay and ....ay with two oral bilabials you will have the words .... and .... If you complete ....ay with the bilabial nasal you will have the word ....

bay   pay

may

/t/   /d/   /n/

50. /   /, /   /, and /   / are alveolar sounds.

/t/   /d/   /n/

51. Two of the alveolars are oral sounds and one is a nasal. /   / and /   / are oral alveolars and /   / is a nasal alveolar.

velar
/k/   /g/
/ŋ/

52. /k/, /g/, and /ŋ/ are the three .... sounds of English. /   / and /   / are orals, whereas /   / is a nasal.

11

mouth	53. When you say /p/, /d/, and /k/, the air stream from your lungs is released through the ....
bilabial alveolar velar orals	54. /b/ is a(n) .... (point of articulation) sound, /t/ is a(n) .... sound, and /g/ is a(n) .... sound; but all three are alike in being ....
/m/ /n/ /ŋ/	55. / / is a bilabial; / / is an alveolar; / / is a velar; but all three are nasals.
completely closed is released through the nose	56. When you say /m/, the lips are .... and the air stream ....
touches the alveolar ridge is released through mouth	57. When you say /d/, the tip of the tongue .... and the air stream ....
touches the velum is released through the nose	58. When you say /ŋ/, the back of the tongue .... and the air stream ....

59. There is one difference between Diagram A and Diagram B, and it represents the major difference in the production of oral and nasal sounds. Find that difference.

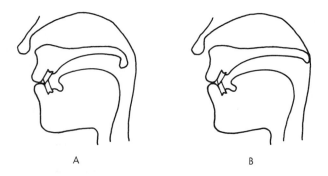

A   B

In B, the velum is raised to block off the nasal cavity. In A, the velum is lowered, thus permitting the air stream to escape through the nasal passage. One of

A

the diagrams represents /b/ and one represents /m/.
Would you guess that A or B represents /m/? ....

raised

60. The velum is .... (*raised* or *lowered*)
during the production of the orals /t, d, p, b, k, g/.

lowered

61. The velum is .... (*raised* or *lowered*)
during the production of the nasals /m, n, ŋ/.

62. The six diagrams below represent the production of
the nine sounds we have studied so far. Taking into
consideration both the point of articulation and the
position of the velum, assign the appropriate symbol(s)
to each diagram.

1) /t/   /d/
2) /ŋ/
3) /n/

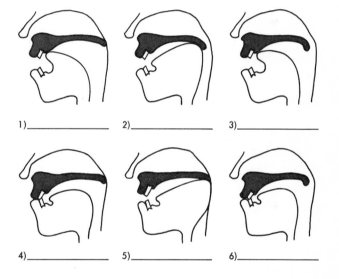

1)_____ 2)_____ 3)_____

4) /p/   /b/
5) /k/   /g/
6) /m/

4)_____ 5)_____ 6)_____

63. The velum is raised during the production of a(n)
.... sound, and it is lowered during the
production of a(n) .... sound.

oral

nasal

64. We symbolize the last phoneme of *bus* as /s/ and the
last phoneme of *buzz* as /z/. But notice again that the
spelling of the sound in writing is not always the same
as the symbol used to represent the sound. What is
the spelling of the phoneme /s/ in each of these words?

a) ce   c) c

b) sc   d) s

a) France ....   c) circle ....

b) scene ....   d) sitting ....

13

65. The sound /z/ occurs in each of the words below. How is it spelled in each case?

a) s   b) se   c) z

a) his ....   b) these ....   c) zipper ....

/s/   /z/

66. *Hiss* ends with /   /; *his* ends with /   /.

67. Try these. Which words end with /s/ and which with /z/?

a) /z/   e) /z/
b) /s/   f) /s/
c) /s/   g) /z/
d) /z/

a) was /   /   e) rose /   /
b) miss /   /   f) loss /   /
c) loose /   /   g) is   /   /
d) lose /   /

68. Say the words *bus* and *buzz*, prolonging the final sound of each word. Is the position of your tongue the same for /s/ and /z/? .... Describe.

yes
The tip (or for some people, the front) of the tongue is near (but not touching) the alveolar ridge.

....

....

....

....

69. The point in the mouth where the air stream is modified during the articulation of /s/ and /z/ is the

alveolar ridge

.... ; therefore, /s/ and /z/ are alveolars.

/t/   /d/   /n/   /s/   /z/

70. /   /, /   /, /   /, /   /, and /   / are all alveolars.

orals

71. Are /s/ and /z/ orals or nasals? ....
Explain.

The air stream is released through the mouth.

....

....

14

/m/   /n/   /ŋ/

72. There are only three nasals in English and they are /   /, /   /, and /   /.

velum
nose

73. During the production of /m/, /n/, and /ŋ/, the .... is lowered and the air stream passes unhindered through the .... But during the production of oral sounds, the air stream can be released in several different ways, depending on how it is interfered with as it passes through the mouth. /t/ and /d/ represent one manner of oral release of air; /s/ and /z/ represent another. As you start to say /t/ and /d/, the tongue presses firmly against the alveolar ridge, completely stopping the air stream. Then, when the tongue leaves the alveolar ridge, the air stream is expelled. If you say /t/ and /d/ you will feel the complete blockage of the air stream followed by the air release. Sounds articulated in this way are called **stops**. At some point during the articulation of a stop, the air stream is completely blocked. Say /p/ and /b/. Are these phonemes stops? .... Why?

yes
Because the air stream is completely blocked and then released.

74. Now say /s/ and /z/. Are these phonemes stops? .... Explain.

no
The air stream is not completely blocked.

75. At no time during the articulation of /s/ and /z/ is the air stream completely blocked. When you say /s/ and /z/ you can feel that the air stream passes continuously through a narrow opening in the mouth. /s/ and /z/ belong to the group of oral sounds called **fricatives**. During the articulation of a fricative, there is friction as the air stream passes continuously through the constricted opening in the mouth. /t/ and /d/ are alveolar stops. /s/ and /z/ are ....

alveolar
fricatives

15

no
During the production of
these sounds the air stream
does not continue
uninterrupted through a
narrow opening.
[or] When these sounds are
produced, the air stream is
completely blocked.

76. /b/, /p/, /k/, and /g/ are all oral sounds. Are they fricatives? .... Explain.

....

....

....

....

....

....

....

....

77. Nasal, stop, and fricative name three **manners of articulation**, three different ways that air is released during the articulation of a sound. The manner of articulation for /m/ is nasal; that is, when /m/ is articulated, the air stream ....

is released through the nose

....

The manner of articulation for /p/ is stop; that is, when /p/ is articulated, the air stream ....

is completely blocked and
then released through the
mouth

....

And the manner of articulation for /z/ is fricative; that is, when /z/ is articulated, the air stream ....

passes through a narrow or
constricted opening in the
mouth

....

/m/   /n/
/ŋ/   /p/
/b/   /t/   /d/   /k/   /g/
fricatives

78. The three nasals of English are /   /, /   /, and /   /. The stops we have studied so far are /   /, /   /, /   /, /   /, /   /, and /   /. /s/ and /z/ are ....

bilabial
stop

alveolar   stops
alveolar
fricatives
velar   stops

79. /p/ and /b/ have the same point of articulation (................................) and the same manner of articulation (................................). /t/ and /d/ have the same point and manner of articulation; they are both .... (point) .... (manner), /s/ and /z/ are both .... (point) .... (manner), and /k/ and /g/ are both .... (point) .... (manner). Yet we recognize that /p/ and /b/, /t/ and /d/, /s/ and /z/, and /k/ and /g/ are different phonemes

16

despite the fact that the members of each pair of sounds have the same point and manner of articulation. Some additional feature must distinguish /p/ from /b/, /t/ from /d/, /s/ from /z/, and /k/ from /g/. That distinguishing feature is most readily apparent in the production of /s/ and /z/.

80. Pronounce /s/ and /z/ in rapid succession; that is, /s-z-s-z-s-z-s-z/. While you continue pronouncing these sounds, place your fingertips on your throat (Adam's apple). You will notice that during the pronunciation of /z/ you can feel the vibration of the **vocal cords**. This vibration is called **voicing**, and sounds that have this accompanying vibration are called **voiced sounds**. The last sound of *buzz* (/z/) is a **voiced sound**. The last sound of *bus* (/s/) is a **voiceless sound**; that is, it is not accompanied by vibration of the vocal cords. Are the last sounds of *was*, *eyes*, and *Liz* voiced

voiced

or voiceless? .... Are the last sounds of *miss*, *pass*, and *ice* voiced or voice-

voiceless

less? ....

81. Pronounce each of the following words, prolonging or exaggerating the final sound in each, then indicate whether it is voiced (vd) or voiceless (vl):

a) vl	d) vl	g) vl
b) vd	e) vl	h) vl
c) vd	f) vd	i) vd

a) toss	d) less	g) sauce ....
b) cause	e) peace	h) choice ....
c) maze	f) peas	i) phrase ....

82. The words *cap* and *cab* end with the bilabial stops

/p/   /b/

/   / and /   /. Which of these two is voiceless?

/p/   /b/

/   / Which is voiced? /   /

83. The words *cat* and *cad* end with the alveolar stops /t/

/t/

and /d/. Which of the two is voiceless? /   /

/d/

Which is voiced? /   /

84. The words *back* and *bag* end with the velar stops /k/

/k/

and /g/. Which sound is voiceless? /   / Which

/g/

is voiced? /   /

17

/p/   /b/
/t/   /d/   /k/   /g/

/b/   /d/
/g/   /p/   /t/
/k/

/m/   /n/
/ŋ/

voiced

nasal

all nasals of English are
voiced

/b/   /d/   /g/
/p/   /t/   /k/
/z/
/s/

A
B

85. Notice that the six stops fall into three vl/vd pairs; a bilabial pair /   / and /   /; an alveolar pair /   / and /   /; and a velar pair /   / and /   /.

86. The voiced stops of English are /   /, /   /, and /   /, and the voiceless stops are /   /, /   /, and /   /.

87. Pronounce the three words *some*, *sun*, and *sung*. The last sounds in these words are the nasals /   /, /   /, and /   /. Pronounce each word again, exaggerating the last sound in each. Are they all voiced or voiceless?
....

88. All three .... sounds are voiced.

89. It is never necessary to describe an English phoneme as a *voiced* nasal because ....
....

90. But voicing is often used to distinguish one stop or fricative from another because some stops are voiced (like /   /, /   /, and /   /), and some are voiceless (like /   /, /   /, and /   /). And some fricatives are voiced (like /   /), and some are voiceless (like /   /).

91. A more complete facial diagram than we have used so far could indicate voicing by drawing a wavy line (∼) in the throat of the diagram to represent voicing and a straight line (—) to represent absence of voicing. Following such a suggestion, which diagram below would represent /g/? .... Which would represent /k/? ....

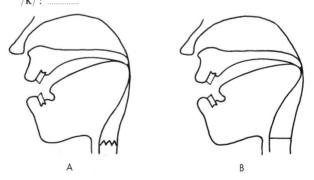

A   B

18

no
The lips do not close nor
come completely together.

92. Are the first sound of *fine* (/f/) and the first sound of *vine* (/v/) bilabials? .... Explain. ....
....
....

The lower lip touches the
upper teeth.

93. Describe the position of your lower lip and upper teeth when you say /f/ and /v/.
....
....

touching the upper front
teeth with the lower lip

94. /f/ and /v/ are the two **labiodental sounds** (or simply **labiodentals**) of English; that is, they are the two sounds that are made by ....
....
....

Study the diagram below:

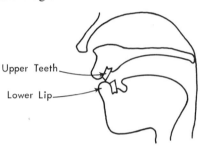

Upper Teeth
Lower Lip

/s/

95. Is the manner of articulation of /f/ and /v/ like that of /p/ or /s/ or /ŋ/? It is like /   /.

/f/   /v/
fricative

96. The manner of articulation for the two labiodental phonemes of English (/   / and /   /) is ....
.... (*nasal*, *stop*, or *fricative*).

passes through a narrow or
constricted opening in the
mouth

97. During the production of /f/ and /v/, the air stream
....
....
....

98. The two labiodentals have the same point of articulation and they are both fricatives. But since we easily distinguish such words as *fine* and *vine*, we know

19

that /f/ and /v/ are different phonemes. What is the difference between them? /f/ is .... and /v/ is ....

voiceless
voiced

99. Is the first sound in *thy* the same as the first sound in *thigh*? ....

no

100. The two English words *thy* and *thigh*, in spite of their spellings, are pronounced exactly the same way except for the first sound in each word. Pronounce them. The difference between these two initial sounds is the same that we found between /f/ and /v/: One is .... and the other is ....

voiceless
voiced

101. Exaggerate or prolong the initial sounds in *thy* and *thigh*. Which word begins with a voiceless sound? .... Which one with a voiced sound? ....

thigh
thy

102. We use the symbol /ð/ for the first sound (spelled *th*) of *thy* and /θ/ for the first sound (also spelled *th*) of *thigh*. That is, /ð/ represents the voiced sound and /θ/ the voiceless sound. Here are some additional words that begin with these phonemes. Pronounce them and decide which of the two phonemes is represented in each of the words.

a) /θ/   f) /ð/
b) /θ/   g) /θ/
c) /θ/   h) /ð/
d) /ð/   i) /θ/
e) /ð/

a) thin   /   /   f) those   /   /
b) thank   /   /   g) thistle /   /
c) thumb   /   /   h) the   /   /
d) than   /   /   i) thought /   /
e) there   /   /

103. Answer these questions concerning the articulation of /θ/ and /ð/.

   a) Do they have the same point of articulation? ....

a) yes
b) no
c) no
d) no
e) yes
f) no

   b) Are they both voiced sounds? ....
   c) Are they both voiceless sounds? ....
   d) Are they stops? ....
   e) Are they fricatives? ....
   f) Are they nasals? ....

20

no
no

104. /θ/ and /ð/ have the same point of articulation. Are /θ/ and /ð/ bilabials? .... Are they labio-dentals? ....

The upper teeth and lower lip do not touch when /θ/ and /ð/ are produced.

105. How do you know that /θ/ and /ð/ are not labio-dentals? ....
....
....

106. /θ/ and /ð/ are the two **interdental sounds** (or simply **interdentals**) of English. Prolong the pronunciation of /θ/ in *thin*. Describe the position of your tongue and teeth in making this interdental. ....
....
....

The tip of the tongue is between the upper and lower teeth.

Now look at the diagram.

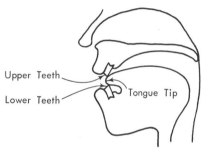

/ð/
/θ/

107. The voiced interdental is represented by / /. The voiceless interdental is represented by / /.

raised (See the diagram in Frame 59.)
mouth

108. During the production of /θ/ and /ð/, the velum is .... (*raised* or *lowered*), thus block-ing off the nasal passage so the air stream is released through the ....

/θ/
/ð/
the air stream passes through a narrow opening in the mouth

109. The voiceless interdental / / and the voiced inter-dental / / are oral sounds. We call them inter-dental fricatives because ....
....
....

/θ/   /ð/

/t/

110. We have seen that the spelling *th* can represent both the / / sound of *thin* and the / / sound of *then*. It can also represent the first sound of *Thomas* which is / /.

21

point

111. Interdental names the .... of articulation of /θ/ and /ð/, and fricative names their

manner

.... of articulation.

interdental

112. /θ/ and /ð/ are the two ....

fricatives

(point of articulation) ....

(manner of articulation) of English.

SUMMARY OF FRAMES 48–112

We have considered several important features in describing English phonemes. In the first section we were mainly concerned with points of articulation: At what point in the oral cavity is the air stream modified during the articulation of a particular sound? In the last section we considered the manner of articulation of some sounds: When we produce a certain sound, is the velum lowered so that the air stream is released through the nose (producing a nasal)? Or is it raised, thus blocking off the nasal passage so that the air stream is released through the mouth (thus producing an oral)? And if released through the mouth, then is the air stream continuous in its passage (fricative), or is it temporarily blocked at some point (stop)?

Voicing is another significant feature in the description of a sound. When a given speech sound is articulated, are the vocal cords vibrating (producing a voiced sound) or are they at rest (producing a voiceless sound)?

So far, we have studied five points of articulation: bilabial (/p, b, m/), alveolar (/t, d, n, s, z/), velar (/k, g, ŋ/), labiodental (/f, v/), and interdental (/θ, ð/). We have also studied three manners of articulation: nasal, stop, and fricative.

Now you are ready to start filling in the consonant chart on page 61. Before going on to Section 3, turn to page 61 and write the appropriate phonemic symbols in squares 1–15. Then check your chart with answers 1–15 on page 62. When you have finished 1–15 on the consonant chart, begin Section 3.

SECTION 3

In Section 3 you will study six new English phonemes, one new point of articulation, and three new manners of articulation. By the end of this section you will be able to:

a) identify six more English phonemes and write the symbol for each;
b) describe six more English phonemes in terms of voicing and their point and manner of articulation;
c) label and describe one new point of articulation;
d) label and describe three new manners of articulation;
e) list twenty-one English phonemes (all those studied by the end of Section 3) in appropriate categories of voicing, and point and manner of articulation.

---

113. We represent the first phoneme in *see*, *sip*, and *sin* as /s/. The first phoneme in *she*, *ship*, and *shin* we represent by one symbol /š/. Notice that /š/ represents one phoneme, although this single phoneme is often

sh

spelled in English with the two letters .... (However, the phoneme /š/ is not always spelled this way: e.g., *sugar*, *sure*, **Chicago**, *motion*, *passion*, *machine*.) Substitute /š/ for the first phoneme in the words given below and write the new words.

a) sheet   d) shame
b) show   e) sheep
c) shoe

a) seat ....   d) same ....
b) so   ....   e) seep ....
c) Sue   ....

114. Pronounce /s/ and /š/. As you go from the first to the second of these sounds, does your tongue move toward the front of the mouth or toward the back?

toward the back

....

115. We have learned that /s/ is a voiceless alveolar fricative. This simply means that the air stream is maximally constricted (not completely stopped) at the alveolar ridge and that the vocal cords are not vibrating. The /š/ phoneme is very similar to /s/ but differs from it in one main feature:

yes   Are both /s/ and /š/ voiceless? ....
yes   Are both /s/ and /š/ fricatives? ....
no   Are both /s/ and /š/ alveolars? ....

23

116. When /s/ is produced, the point of maximum constriction is the alveolar ridge. When /š/ is produced,
the point of maximum constriction is not the alveolar
ridge but a point immediately behind it in what is
called the **alveopalatal** area. Sounds produced at this
point are called **alveopalatal sounds,** or just **alveo-
palatals**. /s/ is a voiceless alveolar fricative. /š/ is a

voiceless   alveopalatal
fricative

....

....

117. Pronounce *see* and *she*. Prolong the first sound in
each word. What difference do you notice in the shape
of the lips? ....

The lips are protruded
during the production of /š/
in *she*, but not during the
production of /s/.

....

....

118. Like /f/, /θ/, and /s/, /š/ is .... (*vd* or *vl*) and
it is a .... (*stop* or *fricative*).

vl
fricative

119. The oral sounds we have studied so far can be described
in pairs having one voiced and one voiceless member.
There is a pair of bilabial stops. /   / is voiceless;
/   / is voiced. There is a pair of labiodental
fricatives. /   / is voiceless; /   / is voiced. There
is a pair of interdental fricatives. /   / is voiceless;
/   / is voiced. There is a pair of alveolar stops.
/   / is voiceless; /   / is voiced. There is a pair
of alveolar fricatives. /   / is voiceless; /   / is
voiced. There is a pair of velar stops. /   / is voiceless; /   / is voiced.

/p/
/b/
/f/   /v/
/θ/
/ð/
/t/   /d/
/s/   /z/
/k/
/g/

120. Like these other oral sounds, the ....
(point) /š/ has a voiced counterpart /ž/, as in *pleasure*,
illusion, and *azure*.

alveopalatal

121. Every word listed below contains either /š/ or /ž/.
Pronounce each word slowly, then indicate which
phoneme it contains.

a) /š/   d) /ž/
b) /š/   e) /š/
c) /ž/

a) emotion /   /   d) vision /   /
b) pressure /   /   e) shred /   /
c) delusion /   /

/š/	122. During the production of the two alveopalatals / /
/ž/	and / /, the air is released through a constricted
	opening at the alveopalatal area behind the alveolar
	ridge.

alveopalatal	123. /š/ and /ž/ are .... (point)
/š/ /ž/	fricatives. / / is voiceless and / / is voiced.

yes	124. Are /g/ and /ž/ alike in voicing? .... In point
no	of articulation? ....

	125. /v/ and /ž/ are both voiced fricatives, but /v/ is a(n)
labiodental	.... (point), whereas /ž/
alveopalatal	is a(n) .... (point).

	126. The first sound of *chill* (/č/) and the first sound of *Jill*
	(/ǰ/) complete the set of voiced/voiceless pairs of oral
voiceless	sounds in English. /č/ is the ....
voiced	sound; /ǰ/ is the .... sound.

127. Beside each word in the list below, write the symbol
(either /č/ as in *chill* or /ǰ/ as in *Jill*) for the sound
spelled by the underlined letters.

a) /ǰ/	f) /č/	a) e<u>dge</u> / /	f) it<u>ch</u> / /
b) /ǰ/	g) /ǰ/	b) a<u>ge</u> / /	g) <u>j</u>ust / /
c) /ǰ/	h) /č/	c) ju<u>dge</u> / /	h) na<u>t</u>ure / /
d) /č/	i) /ǰ/	d) <u>ch</u>urch / /	i) <u>g</u>em / /
e) /č/	j) /č/	e) mu<u>ch</u> / /	j) fu<u>tu</u>re / /

	128. Is the point of articulation of /č/ and /ǰ/ the same as
yes	the point of articulation of /š/ and /ž/? ....

alveopalatal	129. Like /š/ and /ž/, /č/ and /ǰ/ are ....
	(point) sounds.

/š/ /ž/	130. The four alveopalatals of English are / /, / /,
/č/ /ǰ/	/ /, and / /.

25

131. /č/ and /ǰ/ are a special pair of English sounds that have characteristics of both stops and fricatives. /č/ and /ǰ/ are called **affricates**. /č/ is the voiceless alveopalatal .... /ǰ/ is the ....

....

affricate   voiced
alveopalatal   affricate

132. The affricates (/   / and /   /) can be described as sounds that begin like stops and end like fricatives.

/č/   /ǰ/

133. Let's see if the affricates /č/ and /ǰ/ do begin like stops by comparing them with the stops /t/ and /d/. Start to say *tip*, but don't say it. Start to say *chip*, but don't say it. Does the front of your tongue press against the roof of your mouth, completely blocking the stream of air as you begin both /t/ and /č/? ....

yes

134. Start to say *dip*, but don't say it. Start to say *gyp*, but don't say it. Does the front of your tongue press against the roof of your mouth, completely blocking the stream of air as you begin both /d/ and /ǰ/? ....

yes

135. /č/ and /ǰ/, the only two .... sounds of English, begin like stops. As we start to say /č/ and /ǰ/, the tongue touches the alveopalatal area, completely blocking the stream of air.

affricate

136. To test whether affricates end like fricatives, we can compare the words *mash* and *match*. The last sound of *mash* is the alveopalatal fricative /   /; the last sound in *match* is the alveopalatal affricate /   /.

/š/
/č/

137. Say the pair of words *mash/match* several times. You will feel an unbroken stream of air pass through your mouth when you say the first word, but you will feel a blockage of the stream of air after the vowel sound in the second; that is, at the beginning of the last sound of *match*. During the production of the last sound of *match*, the air stream is blocked when the tongue touches the alveopalatal area or the front of the palate. After your tongue has touched the palate

for the /č/ sound of *match*, it moves away from the palate and the air stream is allowed to continue forward and out the mouth. The sound you hear after the blockage when the air is released is very similar to /š/. Try to say *match* without letting your tongue touch your palate; that is, take the stop part out of the last sound and just leave the fricative part of the sound. If you say *match* without blocking the air stream, the word will not sound like *match*, but more

mash

like .... If you take the stop part out of

shin

the /č/ in the phrase, *your chin*, you'll have the phrase

your .... And if you take the stop part

sheep

out of the /č/ in the sentence, *They're cheap*, you'll have the new sentence, *They're* ....

/ǰ/

138. The last sound in *Madge* is /   /. As you pronounce this word, you will again feel a blockage of the air stream after the vowel. The tongue blocks the air

touching the front of the palate or touching the alveopalatal area

stream by ....

....

....

139. When you say *Madge*, what happens to your tongue and to the stream of air *after* your tongue has touched

The tongue leaves the hard palate and the air stream continues out the mouth.

the hard palate? ....

....

....

140. Say *Madge* without letting your tongue touch your hard palate. The last sound will now be quite like the

/ž/

phoneme /   /.

141. The two affricates of English, (/č/ and /ǰ/), do begin like stops and end like the alveopalatal fricatives

/š/   /ž/

/   / and /   /.

142. For every sound in the following list, indicate (1) whether the sound is voiced or voiceless, (2) the point of articulation, and (3) the manner of articulation (nasal, fricative, stop, affricate).

EXAMPLE: /b/   vd   bilabial   stop

27

vl alveolar fricative	/s/	....
vd velar nasal	/ŋ/	....
vd interdental fricative	/ð/	....
vl velar stop	/k/	....
vd alveopalatal affricate	/ǰ/	....
vl bilabial stop	/p/	....
vl labiodental fricative	/f/	....
vd bilabial nasal	/m/	....
vl alveolar stop	/t/	....
vd alveolar fricative	/z/	....
vd velar stop	/g/	....
vd labiodental fricative	/v/	....
vd alveolar stop	/d/	....
vl alveopalatal affricate	/č/	....
vd alveopalatal fricative	/ž/	....
vd alveolar nasal	/n/	....
vl interdental fricative	/θ/	....
vl alveopalatal fricative	/š/	....

143. What is the initial phoneme in each of the following words? Say each word out loud before making a decision.

EXAMPLE: boy   /b/

28

a) /d/ g) /g/
b) /f/ h) /ǰ/
c) /š/ i) /v/
d) /č/ j) /ð/
e) /θ/ k) /t/
f) /k/

a) dog / / g) gun / /
b) phone / / h) George / /
c) sugar / / i) very / /
d) chalk / / j) than / /
e) thumb / / k) Thomas / /
f) character / /

144. What is the final phoneme in each of the following words? Say each word out loud before making a decision.

EXAMPLE: cab /b/

a) /t/ e) /z/
b) /d/ f) /ǰ/
c) /ŋ/ g) /θ/
d) /š/ h) /č/

a) baked / / e) was / /
b) called / / f) judge / /
c) sing / / g) myth / /
d) fish / / h) match / /

145. /l/ is the first and last sound of the word *lull*. It is the first sound of *lamp* and *leg*; it is the last sound of *pull* and *feel*. Is /l/ a voiced sound? ....

yes

146. The articulation of /l/ is quite different from that of the other sounds we have studied. The tongue tip touches the center of the alveolar ridge and the air stream passes around one or both sides of the tongue. /l/ is called a **lateral sound** (or simply a **lateral**). Giving a more complete description of /l/, we could say /l/ is a

voiced alveolar
lateral

.... (*vd* or *vl*) ....
(point) .... (manner).

147. /l/ is the only English sound during the production of which the air stream is released around the side(s) of the tongue; that is, /l/ is the only ....

lateral

sound.

148. We found earlier that it is unnecessary to refer to a nasal sound as a *voiced* nasal, because all the nasals in English are voiced. The expressions *velar nasal* or *alveolar nasal* or *bilabial nasal* are each sufficient to distinguish one particular English phoneme from the rest. The situation with /l/ is analogous in that it is unnecessary to specify the voicing and the point of

articulation for /l/. Since the manner of air release for /l/ differentiates it from all other English phonemes, we can designate /l/ simply as a ....

lateral

149. The first and last sound of *roar* is called a **retroflex sound** (or simply a **retroflex**). Like /l/, /r/ is different from the other phonemes we have studied in its manner of articulation. When you say /r/, you can feel the sides of your tongue press against your upper teeth (molars). The tip of the tongue may be curled up and back. Does the tip of the tongue touch the roof of the mouth when you say /r/? .... What is the position of your lips when you say /r/?

no

rounded

....

/l/   vd

150. Like the lateral /   /, the retroflex /r/ is a .... (*vd* or *vl*) sound.

vd
retroflex

151. We could describe /r/ as a .... (*vd* or *vl*) .... (manner).

152. Just as /l/ can be unambiguously selected from among all other English phonemes simply by naming its manner of articulation, so it is with /r/. We can identify /l/ simply as the .... We can identify /r/ simply as the ....

lateral

retroflex

SUMMARY OF FRAMES 113–152

When we pronounce /š/, /ž/, /č/, and /ǰ/, the air stream is modified in the alveopalatal area (behind the alveolar ridge). When we pronounce the two alveopalatal fricatives (/š/ and /ž/), the front of the tongue approaches the alveopalatal area, thus forcing the air to scrape through a narrow opening. But the air is released differently when we articulate the alveopalatal affricates /č/ and /ǰ/. When we say /č/ and /ǰ/, the tongue touches the hard palate initially and then drops slightly, allowing the air to continue through the narrowed opening. Affricates combine two manners of articulation that we studied earlier; affricates begin like stops and end like fricatives.

/l/ is the only lateral phoneme in English, the only sound that involves the release of the air stream around one or both sides of the tongue. And /r/, the only English retroflex phoneme, is articulated with the sides of the tongue pressing against the upper teeth (molars).

Now turn again to the consonant chart on page 61. Write the required phonemes in squares 16–21. Remember to check your chart with the answers 16–21 on page 62. Then go to Section 4.

In Section 4 you will study five vowel phonemes. By the end of this section you will be able to:

SECTION 4

a) identify these five vowel phonemes in words;
b) write the phonemic symbol for each;
c) read and write phonemic transcriptions of words containing these five vowel phonemes.

See next frame.

153. How many vowels are there in English? ....

154. Did you answer "five" for the last frame, thinking, "a, e, i, o, u"? Or did you answer "seven," thinking, "a, e, i, o, u, and sometimes y and w"? Either answer shows that you were thinking of how many *letters* we use in English to represent vowel *sounds*. But we are not concerned here with the English spelling system, we are concerned with the *sound* system of English. By pronouncing the following list of words, you can easily see that there are more than five contrastive vowels in English:

beet	bait	bat	boot	bought	bout
bit	bet	but	boat	bite	

Each word in the list begins with /b/ and ends with /t/. By substituting different vowel sounds in the environment /b........t/, how many vowel nuclei have we demonstrated? ....

eleven

vowel nuclei

155. The only difference between *beet* and *bit* is that difference between the .... in the two words.

156. Seven of the vowel nuclei from this /b........t/ word list will also fit into the environment /l........k/ to make sensible English words. Below you are going to write out the /l........k/ words. First *say* the /b........t/ guide word to yourself. Then pronounce the vowel in isolation several times. Say that vowel in the environment /l........k/ and then write the English word.

31

a) leak, leek d) lack
b) lick e) luck
c) lake f) like

EXAMPLE: boot Luke ....

a) beet .... d) bat ....
b) bit .... e) but ....
c) bait .... f) bite ....

There are more vowel nuclei in English than are shown in the above lists of words. For most English speakers, a complete inventory of vowel contrasts would number between twelve and fifteen. As you know, English speakers from different geographical areas vary in their pronunciation. English speakers differ from one another most in the total number of vowel contrasts they use, and in the distribution of those vowels (i.e., the set of words in which they use particular vowels). In the following frames we will try to identify and describe fourteen of the English vowel nuclei.

bait	*bet*
eight	net
rate	bed
may	bread
taste	

157. Some of the words in the list below have the vowel of *bait* and some have the vowel of *bet*. In the first column, write the words with the vowel of *bait*. In the second column write the words that contain the vowel of *bet*.

	bait	*bet*
eight	....	....
net	....	....
rate	....	....
may	....	....
bed	....	....
bread	....	....
taste	....	....

a) /ey/ h) /ey/
b) /e/ i) /ey/
c) /e/ j) /e/
d) /ey/ k) /ey/
e) /e/ l) /ey/
f) /ey/ m) /ey/
g) /e/

158. We use the symbol /ey/ to represent the vowel nucleus of *bait* and the symbol /e/ for the vowel nucleus of *bet*. Beside each word below write the appropriate symbol for the vowel it contains.

EXAMPLE: age /ey/ edge /e/

a) mate / / h) date / /
b) met / / i) lace / /
c) pest / / j) less / /
d) paste / / k) made / /
e) men / / l) day / /
f) main / / m) maid / /
g) debt / /

159. As the symbols /ey/ and /e/ suggest, these two vowel nuclei differ in complexity. Repeat the words *bait* and *bet* several times, exaggerating the vowel sound in each. You will notice that during the pronunciation of the /ey/ of *bait* there is a change in vowel quality; that is, the vowel begins with a sound similar to that of the /e/ in *bet* but ends with a sound similar to the vowel sound in *beet*. We call vowels that have this characteristic of changing quality during their production **complex** vowels. The vowel quality of *bet*, /e/, is relatively static from beginning to end. We call vowels that have this characteristic **simple** vowels. /e/ is a .... vowel. /ey/ is a .... vowel.

simple   complex

160. If you put the vowel /ey/ in the environment /f.......l/ you get the word ....

fail

161. If you put the vowel /e/ in the environment /t.......l/ you get the word ....

tell

162. /ey/ is a .... vowel and /e/ is a .... vowel.

complex
simple

163. The vowel sounds of *bid* and *bead* form another simple-complex pair. We represent the vowel of *bid* by the symbol /i/, and the vowel of *bead* with /iy/. Beside each word below, write the symbol of the vowel it contains.

EXAMPLE: eat   /iy/   it   /i/

a) /iy/   g) /iy/
b) /i/   h) /i/
c) /i/   i) /iy/
d) /iy/   j) /iy/
e) /i/   k) /iy/
f) /iy/   l) /i/

a) heed   /   /   g) piece   /   /
b) hid   /   /   h) thing   /   /
c) is   /   /   i) shield   /   /
d) ease   /   /   j) cede   /   /
e) ship   /   /   k) peace   /   /
f) sheep   /   /   l) miss   /   /

164. If you put /iy/ in the environment /č.......p/ you get the English word ....

cheap

sin   simple

complex

165. If you put /i/ in the environment /s.........n/ you get the English word .... /i/ is a .... vowel and /iy/ is a .... vowel.

166. Systematically representing the sounds of words with symbols rather than with letters of the alphabet is called transcribing. Words, phrases, and sentences written in sound symbols are called **transcriptions**.

transcription
/beyt/ is the .... of *bait*.

167. The four words *lead* (as in *to lead*), *lid*, *laid*, and *led* differ only in their vowel nuclei. Write the correct word beside each transcription below.

a) lid

b) laid

c) led

d) lead

a) /lid/ ....

b) /leyd/ ....

c) /led/ ....

d) /liyd/ ....

168. Now transcribe the same four words.

a) /liyd/   c) /leyd/

b) /lid/   d) /led/

a) lead /   /   c) laid /   /

b) lid   /   /   d) led /   /

169. /i/ and /e/ are simple vowels. During the pronunciation of these two vowels, the vowel quality ....

doesn't change

170. /iy/ and /ey/ are complex vowels. During the pronunciation of /iy/ and /ey/, the vowel quality ....

changes

171. You are familiar with all the phonemes in the words below and with their symbols. Transcribe these words.

EXAMPLE: bait   /beyt/

a) /frey/   g) /peynt/

b) /eyt/   h) /ney/

c) /šeyk/   i) /eyt/

d) /ðey/   j) /pleyn/

e) /ney/   k) /reyn/

f) /reyn/   l) /pleyn/

a) fray /   /   g) paint /   /

b) eight /   /   h) neigh /   /

c) shake /   /   i) ate   /   /

d) they /   /   j) plane /   /

e) nay   /   /   k) reign /   /

f) rain   /   /   l) plain /   /

172. Each set below has four words, one of which contains the vowel /iy/, one /i/, one /ey/, and one /e/. Transcribe the vowel of each word:

1. a) /i/
   b) /iy/
   c) /ey/
   d) /e/

2. a) /iy/
   b) /e/
   c) /i/
   d) /ey/

3. a) /ey/
   b) /iy/
   c) /i/
   d) /e/

4. a) /ey/
   b) /e/
   c) /iy/
   d) /i/

5. a) /e/
   b) /iy/
   c) /ey/
   d) /i/

6. a) /ey/.
   b) /i/
   c) /e/
   d) /iy/

1. a) big   /   /
   b) cheese   /   /
   c) play   /   /
   d) bed   /   /

2. a) breathe /   /
   b) breath /   /
   c) twig   /   /
   d) slate   /   /

3. a) take   /   /
   b) reach   /   /
   c) king   /   /
   d) met   /   /

4. a) way   /   /
   b) lend   /   /
   c) leave   /   /
   d) this   /   /

5. a) said   /   /
   b) teeth   /   /
   c) wait   /   /
   d) wish   /   /

6. a) weight /   /
   b) inch   /   /
   c) sled   /   /
   d) seed   /   /

173. Do you recognize the words transcribed below? Beside each transcription, write out the word as it is normally spelled.

a) bet
b) bit
c) beat, beet
d) bait
e) reed, read
f) red, read
g) raid
h) rid

a) /bet/ ....
b) /bit/ ....
c) /biyt/ ....
d) /beyt/ ....
e) /riyd/ ....
f) /red/ ....
g) /reyd/ ....
h) /rid/ ....

174. Can you transcribe these words? Try it!

a) /θriy/
b) /čeyn/
c) /šriŋk/
d) /fiyt/
e) /steyd/
f) /spred/
g) /briŋ/
h) /streč/
i) /šiyp/
j) /ðey/
k) /tent/

a) three   /   /
b) chain   /   /
c) shrink /   /
d) feet   /   /
e) stayed /   /
f) spread /   /
g) bring /   /
h) stretch/   /
i) sheep /   /
j) they /   /
k) tent /   /

175. /iy/ and /ey/ are complex (rather than simple) vowels because during their production ....
....

the quality of the vowel changes

176. Some of the words below contain /iy/, some /i/, some /ey/, some /e/. Some of the words below contain none of these. Put each word in one of the columns, depending on which vowel it contains. If a word

35

contains none of the four vowels we have studied so far (/i, iy, ey, e/), list it at the right.

string, map, still, tree, add, sat,
make, bed, brag, egg, reach, mean, trade

/i/	/iy/	/ey/
string still	tree reach mean	make trade

/e/	Other
bed egg	map add sat brag

/i/	/iy/	/ey/	/e/	Other

177. Do these words—*map, add, sat, brag*—have the same

yes

vowel? .... If you put the vowel of *map, add, sat,* and *brag* in the environment /b........t/ you will have

bat

the word ....

178. The transcription of *bat* is /bæt/. The symbol for the

/æ/

vowel phoneme of *bat* is / /. Circle the words in this list that contain /æ/.

chat	lag	man	noise	than	pad	trick	brat	man	fought
than	brat	that	been	treat	say	hut	suit	hope	trot
pad	thank		chat	threat	lag	how	thank	that	my

chat   lag   man
than   brat   that
pad   thank

noise than pad trick brat man fought
been treat say hut suit hope trot
chat threat lag how thank that my

179. Transcribe these words:

a) /čæt/   e) /θæŋk/
b) /ðæt/   f) /pæd/
c) /bræt/   g) /læg/
d) /mæn/   h) /ðæn/

a) chat /   / e) thank /   /
b) that /   / f) pad /   /
c) brat /   / g) lag /   /
d) man /   / h) than /   /

180. So far we have studied five vowel nuclei: /iy/ as in the

beat, beet   bit   bait
bet   bat

word b........t, /i/ as in b........t, /ey/ as in b........t, /e/ as in b........t, and /æ/ as in b........t.

181. The five vowels we have worked on so far will all fit in the environments /l........d/, /m........t/, and /b........d/, which are given in the two columns below. Write the word in the space provided beside the transcription.

36

a) lead   i) mate
b) lad   j) meet, meat
c) lid   k) bad
d) led   l) bead
e) laid   m) bade
f) mat   n) bed
g) mitt   o) bid
h) met

a) /liyd/ ....   i) /meyt/ ....
b) /læd/ ....   j) /miyt/ ....
c) /lid/ ....   k) /bæd/ ....
d) /led/ ....   l) /biyd/ ....
e) /leyd/ ....   m) /beyd/ ....
f) /mæt/ ....   n) /bed/ ....
g) /mit/ ....   o) /bid/ ....
h) /met/ ....

182. Give the symbol for the vowel in each of the following words:

a) /æ/   d) /e/
b) /ey/   e) /iy/
c) /i/

a) drab / /   d) thread / /
b) play / /   e) knee / /
c) spin / /

183. Pronounce the word given on the left; then identify the transcribed word that has the same vowel.

EXAMPLE: pit   a) /mit/   b) /miyt/   a

1) b   1) leg   a) /bæg/   b) /beg/ ....
2) b   2) scratch   a) /piyč/   b) /pæč/ ....
3) a   3) preach   a) /iyč/   b) /eč/ ....
4) a   4) late   a) /eyt/   b) /it/ ....
5) b   5) claim   a) /tiym/   b) /teym/ ....
6) b   6) kicked   a) /pækt/   b) /pikt/ ....
7) b   7) hang   a) /riŋ/   b) /ræŋ/ ....
8) a   8) weep   a) /šiyp/   b) /šeyp/ ....
9) b   9) head   a) /biyd/   b) /bed/ ....
10) a   10) slick   a) /pik/   b) /piyk/ ....
11) a   11) chain   a) /reyn/   b) /ræn/ ....
12) a   12) creep   a) /sliyp/   b) /slip/ ....
13) a   13) trim   a) /lim/   b) /leym/ ....
14) b   14) gal   a) /peyl/   b) /pæl/ ....
15) a   15) cheat   a) /siyt/   b) /sæt/ ....
16) a   16) that   a) /pæt/   b) /pet/ ....
17) a   17) skid   a) /rid/   b) /red/ ....
18) a   18) sled   a) /ded/   b) /did/ ....
19) b   19) shell   a) /teyl/   b) /tel/ ....
20) b   20) paid   a) /šed/   b) /šeyd/ ....

Most English speakers use between twelve and fifteen contrastive vowel nuclei when they speak. The English vowel phonemes include:

/iy/, the vowel sound in *beet*,
/i/, the vowel sound in *bit*,
/ey/, the vowel sound in *bait*,
/e/, the vowel sound in *bet*, and
/æ/, the vowel sound in *bat*.

/i/, /e/, and /æ/ are simple vowels, for during their production the vowel quality remains relatively constant. But /iy/ and /ey/ are complex vowels; that is, the quality of the vowel changes during their pronunciation.

In Section 5 you will study three more vowel nuclei. By the
end of this section you will be able to:

SECTION 5

a) identify these three new vowels in words;
b) write the symbol for each;
c) read and write transcriptions of words containing these
    three vowels.

---

184. When a doctor wants to examine your throat, he says,
     "Open your mouth and say 'ah.'" We represent the
     sound that is often written *ah* with the symbol /a/. The
     phoneme /a/ occurs in these words: *odd, cot, pond, tot,
     nod, not, sod.* Transcribe them:

a) /ad/	e) /nad/	a) / / e) / /
b) /kat/	f) /nat/	b) / / f) / /
c) /pand/	g) /sad/	c) / / g) / /
d) /tat/		d) / /

185. Do these three words all contain /a/: *stock, hatch,*
     notch? ....

no

186. *Stock* and *notch* contain the vowel /   /. *Hatch*
     contains the vowel /   /.

/a/
/æ/

187. Put /a/ in the following environments and write the
     resulting words in the spaces provided.

a) stop	d) box	a) /st......p/ .... d) /b......ks/ ....
b) clock	e) throb	b) /kl......k/ .... e) /θr......b/ ....
c) trod	f) shot	c) /tr......d/ .... f) /š......t/ ....

188. Transcribe these words:

a) /šæks/	g) /bam/	a) shacks / / g) bomb / /
b) /šaks/	h) /čæns/	b) shocks / / h) chance / /
c) /nak/	i) /θæŋk/	c) knock / / i) thank / /
d) /næk/	j) /šap/	d) knack / / j) shop / /
e) /map/	k) /læbz/	e) mop / / k) labs / /
f) /mæp/		f) map / /

189. Pronounce the following pairs of words:

odd	cot	pond	tot
awed	caught	pawned	taught

not	sod	nod
nought	sawed	gnawed

Do you pronounce the two words of each of these pairs differently? ....

....

Most English speakers do, but some do not.

190. The words *odd, cot, pond, tot, not,* and *sod* all contain the vowel / /. For most English speakers, the words *awed, caught, pawned, taught, gnawed, nought,* and *sawed* contain a vowel sound we represent as /ɔ/. The transcription of *tot* is / /. The transcription of *taught* is / /.

/a/

/tat/
/tɔt/

191. What words are these?

a) nod   h) taught
b) gnawed   i) nought
c) pond   j) sawed
d) pawned   k) odd
e) caught   l) cot
f) sod   m) awed
g) not   n) tot

a) /nad/ ....   h) /tɔt/ ....
b) /nɔd/ ....   i) /nɔt/ ....
c) /pand/ ....   j) /sɔd/ ....
d) /pɔnd/ ....   k) /ad/ ....
e) /kɔt/ ....   l) /kat/ ....
f) /sad/ ....   m) /ɔd/ ....
g) /nat/ ....   n) /tat/ ....

192. If you look at the spellings of the /ɔ/ words, you'll notice that the phoneme /ɔ/ is often spelled with the letters .... or .... or ....

aw   au   ou

193. The /ɔ/ sound in the words below is not spelled *aw, au,* or *ou.* Transcribe these /ɔ/ words.

a) /bɔl/   f) /rɔŋ/
b) /kɔst/   g) /tɔk/
c) /sɔlt/   h) /brɔθ/
d) /lɔŋ/   i) /sɔft/
e) /krɔs/

a) ball /   /   f) wrong /   /
b) cost /   /   g) talk /   /
c) salt /   /   h) broth /   /
d) long /   /   i) soft /   /
e) cross /   /

194. Write these words in the correct column below: *cot, odd, cat, sod, caught, awed, add, sad, sawed.*

/æ/	/a/	/ɔ/

/æ/	/a/	/ɔ/
cat	cot	caught
add	odd	awed
sad	sod	sawed

195. Which word in each group below contains /ɔ/? Write the word and then transcribe it below.

a) cloth   /klɔθ/

b) fought   /fɔt/

c) pause   /pɔz/

d) draw   /drɔ/

e) fall   /fɔl/

a) act   cloth   lit   dot   a) ....
                                     /   /

b) sock   tan   fought   main   b) ....
                                     /   /

c) pause   Tom   came   sheer   c) ....
                                     /   /

d) brick   draw   let   crop   c) ....
                                     /   /

e) hip   said   got   fall   e) ....
                                     /   /

196. The vowel sound in the words *boat, code,* and *no* is another complex vowel. Pronounce the word *no,* prolonging the vowel. You will notice that the vowel begins with one quality but ends with a vowel sound similar to the vowel in *new.* We transcribe this complex vowel with the complex symbol /ow/. Circle the words below which contain /ow/:

know   wrote
sew   loan
toe

a) know   e) look
b) not   f) rot
c) sew   g) wrote
d) toe   h) loan

41

197. What words are these? Write the word beside the transcription given.

a) note   h) goat

b) shone,   i) soul,
   shown   sole

c) coast   j) tone

d) moan   k) mope

e) close   l) throat

f) close   m) comb

g) foam

a) /nowt/ ....   h) /gowt/ ....

b) /šown/ ....   i) /sowl/ ....

c) /kowst/ ....   j) /town/ ....

d) /mown/ ....   k) /mowp/ ....

e) /klows/ ....   l) /θrowt/ ....

f) /klowz/ ....   m) /kowm/ ....

g) /fowm/ ....

198. Which words from the following list contain /ow/? Circle them.

None should be circled.

cot	thought	too	hook	song	south
about	box		down	loss	moon	would

199. Put /ow/ in each of the environments given and write the resulting word in the space provided.

a) folks   d) thrown,

b) own   throne

c) soak   e) comb

a) /f.......ks/ ....   d) /θr.......n/ ....

b) /.......n/ ....

c) /s.......k/ ....   e) /k.......m/ ....

SUMMARY OF FRAMES 184–199

We have added three more vowel nuclei to our inventory. The simple vowels /a/ (the vowel sound in *cot*) and /ɔ/ (the vowel sound in *caught*) and the complex vowel /ow/ (the vowel sound in *coat*).

SECTION 6

In this section we will consider three additional vowel phonemes. When you have completed this section you will be able to:

a) identify these three new vowels in words;
b) write the symbol for each;
c) read and write transcriptions of words containing these three vowels.

---

200. Some of the words in the list below contain the vowel sound that is in *fool*, *Luke*, and *pool*. The others contain the vowel of *full*, *look*, and *pull*. List the words with the vowel sound of *fool* in Column A and those with the vowel sound of *full* in Column B.

foot	woman	you	shook	suit	womb
took	soup	put	bull	who	flute
grew	good	mood			

A	B

A	B
you	foot
suit	woman
womb	shook
grew	took
soup	put
who	bull
flute	good
mood	

201. The vowel phonemes of *fool* and *full* make another simple-complex pair (like /i/ and /iy/, and /e/ and /ey/). The vowel phoneme of *full* is simple and that of *fool* is complex. The symbol for the vowel of .... (*full* or *fool*) is /u/ and the symbol for the vowel of .... (*full* or *fool*) is /uw/.

full

fool

202. The vowel of *would* is /   /.

/u/

203. Circle every word in the group below that contains /u/.

could   hood
look   brook   put

could	moose	suds	hood	move
look	but	brook	too	put	gun

43

204. Can you read these transcribed words? Write the word beside each transcription.

a) look   f) good
b) Luke   g) cool
c) pull   h) food
d) pool   i) soon
e) foot   j) cook

a) /luk/ ....   f) /gud/ ....
b) /luwk/ ....   g) /kuwl/ ....
c) /pul/ ....   h) /fuwd/ ....
d) /puwl/ ....   i) /suwn/ ....
e) /fut/ ....   j) /kuk/ ....

205. Put /uw/ in the following environments and write the resulting words.

a) food   d) moon
b) sue   e) fruit
c) tool

a) /f......d/ ....   d) /m......n/ ....
b) /s....../ ....   e) /fr......t/ ....
c) /t......l/ ....

206. Put /u/ in the following environments and write the resulting words.

a) foot   d) shook
b) could   e) stood
c) put

a) /f......t/ ....   d) /š......k/ ....
b) /k......d/ ....   e) /st......d/ ....
c) /p......t/ ....

207. Now transcribe these words:

a) /šuwt/   e) /wud/
b) /tuk/   f) /luwz/
c) /guws/   g) /bul/
d) /druwp/   h) /kuwl/

a) shoot /   /   e) wood /   /
b) took /   /   f) lose /   /
c) goose /   /   g) bull /   /
d) droop /   /   h) cool /   /

208. We transcribe *but* as /bət/. Transcribe these words:

a) /jəmp/   d) /bləd/
b) /dəz/   e) /mənθ/
c) /təŋ/   f) /təč/

a) jump /   /   d) blood /   /
b) does /   /   e) month /   /
c) tongue /   /   f) touch /   /

come   front
love   flood
rush   none
mud   bud

209. Circle all the words in the following list that contain /ə/.

come   good   cook   front   none
love   rush   mud   flood   bud

cook   good
/u/

210. The words in the above list that do not have /ə/ are
.... and .... These words have the vowel /   /.

44

211. One word in each row across contains the vowel sound contained in *but*. Circle that word and transcribe it in the space provided at the right.

a) mussed /məst/
b) shun /šən/
c) bun /bən/
d) cut /kət/
e) fun /fən/
f) mud /məd/
g) spun /spən/

a) mist   mussed   most   mast   a) /   /
b) shone   shin   shun   sheen   b) /   /
c) been   bane   boon   bun   c) /   /
d) cut   kit   caught   Kate   d) /   /
e) phone   fawn   fun   fan   e) /   /
f) mood   mud   mad   maid   f) /   /
g) spawn   Spain   spun   spoon   g) /   /

212. Given below are pairs of vowel sounds which, when put into the environments provided, result in separate English words. For example: /ə/ and /uw/ in the environment /m......s/ represent the words *muss* and *moose*. Try these:

a) shut   shoot
b) tune   ton
c) put   putt
d) noon   none
e) could   cud
f) moose   muss
g) son, sun soon
h) tuck   took
i) boot   but

a) /ə/ and /uw/ : /š....t/   = ... and ....
b) /uw/ and /ə/ : /t....n/   = ... and ....
c) /u/ and /ə/ : /p....t/   = ... and ....
d) /uw/ and /ə/ : /n....n/   = ... and ....
e) /u/ and /ə/ : /k....d/   = ... and ....
f) /uw/ and /ə/ : /m....s/   = ... and ....
g) /ə/ and /uw/ : /s....n/   = ... and ....
h) /ə/ and /u/ : /t....k/   = ... and ....
i) /uw/ and /ə/ : /b....t/   = ... and ....

213. Write these sentences out below the transcription.

1) The store is closed.

2) She came at eight.
3) The man sold John's skates.

4) Did it cost much?
5) Did she choose the green dress?

6) Must they be so rude?

7) Does Bob own a phone?

1) /ðə stɔr iz klowzd/
   ....

2) /šiy keym æt eyt/
   ....

3) /ðə mæn sowld ǰanz skeyts/
   ....

4) /did it kɔst məč/
   ....

5) /did šiy čuwz ðə griyn dres/
   ....

6) /məst ðey biy sow ruwd/
   ....

7) /dəz bab own ə fown/
   ....

45

8) They should be there soon.

8) /ðey šud biy ðer suwn/

....

9) /iz it dəl tə duw ðæt/

....

9) Is it dull to do that?

10) /iz šiy in bed æt ten/

....

10) Is she in bed at ten?

214. Circle the word in the first or second column that rhymes with the word in the third column.

1) a	1) a) /šak/	b) /šuk/	1) lock
2) a	2) a) /kowst/	b) /kɔst/	2) toast
3) b	3) a) /druw/	b) /drɔ/	3) straw
4) a	4) a) /lək/	b) /luk/	4) truck
5) a	5) a) /kuk/	b) /kowk/	5) brook
6) b	6) a) /θruw/	b) /θrow/	6) show
7) b	7) a) /sut/	b) /suwt/	7) cute
8) b	8) a) /owt/	b) /ɔt/	8) taught
9) b	9) a) /šud/	b) /šowd/	9) road
10) a	10) a) /pɔnd/	b) /pand/	10) dawned
11) a	11) a) /suwp/	b) /sowp/	11) troop
12) a	12) a) /rat/	b) /rowt/	12) lot
13) b	13) a) /sɔd/	b) /sad/	13) plod
14) b	14) a) /nat/	b) /nət/	14) strut
15) b	15) a) /šuwd/	b) /šud/	15) would
16) b	16) a) /ful/	b) /fɔl/	16) Paul
17) b	17) a) /druwp/	b) /drap/	17) stop
18) a	18) a) /tuk/	b) /tɔk/	18) cook
19) a	19) a) /put/	b) /pat/	19) foot
20) b	20) a) /kəd/	b) /kud/	20) hood
21) b	21) a) /səm/	b) /sam/	21) Tom
22) b	22) a) /gat/	b) /gowt/	22) throat
23) a	23) a) /kəp/	b) /kowp/	23) pup
24) a	24) a) /sɔŋ/	b) /səŋ/	24) long
25) b	25) a) /ruwm/	b) /rəm/	25) thumb
26) a	26) a) /mowst/	b) /məst/	26) ghost
27) a	27) a) /bərn/	b) /bɔrn/	27) turn
28) b	28) a) /tat/	b) /tuwt/	28) flute
29) a	29) a) /tuwl/	b) /tɔl/	29) school
30) b	30) a) /tən/	b) /tuwn/	30) moon

46

215. The words below include all the vowel nuclei you have studied so far. Transcribe them.

a) /bæt/	l) /lik/	a) bat /	/ l) lick / /
b) /bowt/	m) /lak/	b) boat /	/ m) lock / /
c) /bɔt/	n) /lək/	c) but /	/ n) luck / /
d) /bit/	o) /luwk/	d) bit /	/ o) Luke / /
e) /beyt/	p) /læk/	e) bait /	/ p) lack / /
f) /bɔt/	q) /liyk/	f) bought /	/ q) leak / /
g) /bet/	r) /leyk/	g) bet /	/ r) lake / /
h) /buwt/	s) /luk/	h) boot /	/ s) look / /
i) /biyt/	t) /ček/	i) beat /	/ t) check / /
j) /pat/	u) /čɔk/	j) pot /	/ u) chalk / /
k) /put/	v) /čowk/	k) put /	/ v) choke / /

SUMMARY OF FRAMES 200–215

We have added the following three vowel nuclei to our inventory:

/uw/, the vowel sound in *Luke*;

/u/, the vowel sound in *look*, and

/ə/, the vowel sound in *luck*.

In Section 7 you will review the consonant phonemes and you will study the main features of vowel description. When you complete this section, you will be able to:

a) put eleven vowels on a chart according to their tongue position during their production;
b) describe eleven vowel phonemes in terms of front/central/back, high/mid/low tongue position, and lip rounding;
c) compare pairs of vowels in terms of the relative similarity of their tongue positions.

SECTION 7

---

216. Here are the twenty-one consonants we studied earlier.

/t/ /ǰ/ /f/ /m/ /b/ /z/ /l/ /v/ /n/ /r/
/š/ /p/ /č/ /θ/ /d/ /s/ /ð/ /g/ /ŋ/ /ž/ /k/

Let's review them. First group the consonants according to point of articulation. (/l/ and /r/ are already done for you.)

/p/ /b/ /m/	Bilabial	/ / / / / /
/f/ /v/	Labiodental	/ / / /
/θ/ /ð/	Interdental	/ / / /
/l/ /r/ /t/ /d/	Alveolar	/ l / / r / / / / /
/n/ /s/ /z/		/ / / / / /
/š/ /ž/ /č/ /ǰ/	Alveopalatal	/ / / / / / / /
/k/ /g/ /ŋ/	Velar	/ / / / / /

217. Now group them according to their manner of articulation.

/m/ /n/ /ŋ/	Nasal	/ / / / / /
/p/ /b/ /t/	Stop	/ / / / / /
/d/ /k/ /g/		/ / / / / /
/f/ /v/ /θ/ /ð/	Fricative	/ / / / / / /
/s/ /z/ /š/ /ž/		/ / / / / / / /
/č/ /ǰ/	Affricate	/ / / /
/l/	Lateral	/ /
/r/	Retroflex	/ /

48

/b/ /d/ /g/ /v/
/z/ /ž/ /ǰ/ /ð/
/l/ /r/ /m/ /n/ /ŋ/
/p/ /t/ /k/ /f/
/θ/ /s/ /š/ /č/

218. And now group them as voiced or voiceless.

Voiced / / / / / / / /
/ / / / / / /
/ / / / / / / / /
Voiceless / / / / / / /
/ / / / / / /

219. When we studied consonants, we described each consonant phoneme by answering three basic questions:

1) What is the point of articulation? That is, at what point in the mouth is the passage for the escape of the air stream narrowed or completely blocked?

2) What is the manner of articulation? That is, how is the air stream released?

3) Is voicing present? That is, do the vocal cords vibrate during the articulation of the sound?

Each consonant phoneme differs from every other in one, two, or all three of these main features (point of articulation, manner of articulation, voicing). /p/ and /b/ differ from one another in only one of these main features, namely in .... On the other hand, /n/ and /g/ differ from one another in .... and

voicing

point of articulation
manner of articulation (/n/
is alveolar; /g/ is velar; /n/
is a nasal; /g/ is a stop)

....
....
....
....

220. Now let's look at the vowels. What main features distinguish the vowel phonemes from one another? Pronounce the vowel sounds below and circle every one that is voiced.

/i/ /iy/ /ey/ /e/ /æ/ /a/
/ɔ/ /ow/ /uw/ /u/ /ə/

All should be circled.

221. In English the single feature of voicing is never used to distinguish one vowel phoneme from another because ....
....

all English vowels are
voiced.

222. The difference between vowel sounds is determined mainly by the position of the tongue in the mouth. When we describe the production of a particular

vowel sound we consider:

1) The relative **height** of the highest part (or hump) of the tongue.

2) The relative position of the tongue in terms of **frontness** or **backness** in the mouth.

We describe vowel sounds by saying that the highest part of the tongue is farther **front** or **back**, and **higher** or **lower** during the production of one vowel phoneme than it is during the production of another vowel phoneme. The simple vowels /i/, /e/, and /æ/ are front vowels; that is, during the production of these three vowels the highest part of the tongue is in the .... of the mouth. These front vowels can be plotted on a diagram, from the highest to the lowest as follows:

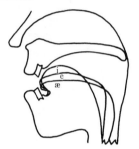

You will be able to feel your jaw—and consequently your tongue—lower as you say *tick* followed immediately by *tack*. Pronounce this pair several times.

223. Both /u/ as in *took* and /ɔ/ as in *talk* are simple back vowels. During the pronunciation of both of these vowels, the highest part of the tongue is in the back of the mouth as indicated in the diagram below. Say *took* and *talk* several times to determine which vowel is high and which is low. Then label the tongue position for /ɔ/ and /u/ in the diagram.

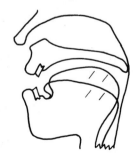

front

/u/

/ɔ/

50

low　　high

224. /ɔ/ is a ....-back vowel. /u/ is a ....
-back vowel.

225. The vowel of *tick* /i/ and the vowel of *took* /u/ are both high vowels. Say these words several times. /u/ is a high-................ vowel, whereas /i/ is a high-................ vowel.

back
front

226. The vowel of *tack* /æ/ and the vowel of *talk* /ɔ/ are both low vowels. Say these vowels several times. /æ/ is a low-................ vowel, whereas /ɔ/ is a low-................ vowel.

front
back

227. This chart can be used to schematically represent the mouth to demonstrate the relative position of the tongue during the pronunciation of vowels. Plot the four vowels /i/, /æ/, /u/, and /ɔ/ on the chart.

	Front	Central	Back
High	/　/		/　/
Mid			
Low	/　/		/　/

/i/		/u/
/æ/		/ɔ/

228. We have already identified the simple front vowel /e/, which is not as .... as /i/ nor as .... as /æ/. Plot it on the chart in Frame 227.

high　　low

/i/		/u/
/e/		
/æ/		/ɔ/

229. We can refer to the vowel /e/ as a mid-................ vowel.

front

51

230. The two remaining simple vowels we have studied are central vowels. They are the vowels of *nut* /ə/ and *not* /a/. One of these vowels is a mid-central vowel and one is a low-central vowel. Say the vowels of *nut* and *not* several times and determine which is the higher:

mid

low

/ə/ is a ....-central vowel.

/a/ is a ....-central vowel.

231. Plot the vowels /ə/ and /a/ on the chart in Frame 227.

/i/		/u/
/e/	/ə/	
/æ/	/a/	/ɔ/

232. Say the highest front vowel and the highest back vowel several times, noticing the position of your lips for each. Are your lips more rounded when you say /i/ or when you say /u/? /   /

/u/

233. Now try the lowest front and back vowels. Are your lips more rounded for /æ/ or for /ɔ/? /   /

/ɔ/

234. "During the articulation of the back vowels of English the lips are rounded." Is this a true statement?

yes

....

no

235. Are any of the front vowels rounded? ....

back

front

236. The .... vowels of English are rounded; the .... vowels of English are unrounded.

237. We have studied four complex vowels, namely /iy/, /ey/, /uw/, and /ow/. These four vowels in the environment /b........t/ would produce the four words

beat   (beet)   bait

boot   boat

.................................., ..., ...,

.................................., and ....

238. The pronunciation of the two complex vowels /iy/ and /ey/ begins with different tongue positions but ends with approximately the same tongue position. This can be tested by the exaggerated pronunciation of *see* and *say*. What element in the transcription of *see* and *say* represents this common tongue position? /   /

/y/

239. The pronunciation of the two complex vowels /uw/ and /ow/ also begins with different tongue positions but ends with approximately the same tongue position. This can be tested by the exaggerated pronunciation of *to* and *toe*. What element in the transcription represents this common tongue position? /   /

/w/

240. If we consider the starting point of the articulation of these four complex vowels, we can describe them as follows:

/iy/ is a high-front vowel.
/ey/ is a mid-front vowel.
/ow/ is a mid-back vowel.
/uw/ is a high-back vowel.

Plot these four vowels in the appropriate square in the chart in Frame 227.

/iy/ /i/		/uw/ /u/
/ey/ /e/	/ə/	/ow/
/æ/	/a/	/ɔ/

241. A teacher of English as a foreign language might say, "My students are having difficulty distinguishing between the high-front vowels." He could say this another way. He could say, "My students are having difficulty distinguishing between /   / and /   /."

/iy/   /i/

242. If his students were having trouble with the low vowels, they would be having trouble with /   /, /   /, and /   /.

/æ/   /a/
/ɔ/

53

243. If he said, "My students have difficulty pronouncing the mid-front vowels," we would understand that his students found / , / and / / troublesome.

/ey/   /e/

244. Every known language has a unique set of contrastive vowels. The set presented here is peculiar to English. In this set, the difference in tongue position during the articulation of certain pairs of vowel phonemes is slight, whereas the difference between other pairs is relatively large. When you articulate /iy/ and /i/, the difference between the two tongue positions is .... (*slight* or *great*). But the difference is much .... (*less* or *greater*) for /uw/ and /æ/ or for /ɔ/ and /iy/.

slight
greater

245. A non-native speaker of English can mispronounce English words in an infinite number of ways, and his mispronunciations will be a result of many factors. However, certain mispronunciations are more likely to occur than others. Students learning English often have difficulty producing accurately those vowel sounds which have relatively close tongue positions, but which function in English as distinctly contrasting sounds. For example, it is not unusual for a non-native speaker of English to pronounce the sentence /ðis iz difikəlt/ as /ðiys iyz diyfiykəlt/. This mispronunciation is due to the substitution of / / for / /, the substitution of one .... (*high-* or *mid-* or *low-*) .... (*front* or *central* or *back*) vowel for the other.

/iy/   /i/
high
front

246. A non-native English speaker, intending to say /luk/, could conceivably substitute the word *Luke* or the word *lock*. *Luke* and *Lock* are both possible mispronunciations of /luk/; however, the substitution .... is less likely because ....
....
....
....
....
....

lock   the tongue
position for /a/ (in *lock*) is
very different from the
tongue position for /u/ (in
look). /a/ is a low central
vowel, whereas /u/ is a high
back vowel

54

Vowel nuclei are described in terms of how high or low and how far front or back the hump of the tongue is when they are articulated. The eleven contrastive vowels we have studied so far include:

> the high-front vowels /iy/ and /i/,
> the mid-front vowels /ey/ and /e/,
> the low-front vowel /æ/,
> the high-back vowels /uw/ and /u/,
> the mid-back vowel /ow/,
> the low-back vowel /ɔ/,
> the mid-central vowel /ə/, and
> the low-central vowel /a/.

Please turn to page 62 and follow these instructions for numbers 1–11:

> 1) Write the appropriate symbol.
> 2) Complete the transcribed word with that symbol.
> 3) Write out the transcribed word on the line provided.

Check your chart with the answers 1–11 on page 62. When you have done this, begin Section 8.

In this section you will study three more complex vowels, three more consonants, and one feature sometimes present in the articulation of certain stops. By the end of this section you will be able to:

SECTION 8

a) identify these three new vowels and three new consonants in words;
b) write the symbol for each;
c) read and write transcriptions of words containing these six new phonemes;
d) place the three vowel phonemes correctly on the vowel chart;
e) name another articulatory feature and recognize its presence or absence in words.

/a/

247. Pronounce the word *pond*. It contains the low-central vowel /   /.

248. Now pronounce the word *pined*. The pronunciation of the vowel nucleus of this word begins with a vowel similar to /a/, that of *pond*, but ends with a sound similar to the last part of the complex vowels /ey/ and /iy/. How do you think the vowel nucleus of *pined*

/ay/

might be transcribed?   /p..........nd/

249. Assign either /a/ or /ay/ to each of the following words:

a) /a/	e) /ay/	a) not / /	e) eye / /
b) /ay/	f) /ay/	b) might / /	f) child / /
c) /ay/	g) /a/	c) time / /	g) crop / /
d) /a/	h) /ay/	d) Tom / /	h) try / /

250. Pronounce the word *pound*. The pronunciation of the vowel nucleus of this word also begins with a vowel sound similar to /a/ but ends with a sound similar to the last part of the complex vowels /ow/ and /uw/. How do you think the vowel nucleus of *pound* will be

/aw/

transcribed?   /p..........nd/

251. All the following words contain the vowel nucleus of *pound*. Transcribe them.

a) /maws/	c) /dawn/	a) mouse / / c) down / /
b) /kaw/	d) /mawθ/	b) cow / / d) mouth / /

56

252. The low-central tongue position is the starting point for one simple vowel, / /, and two complex vowels, / / and / /.

/a/
/ay/ and /aw/

253. If we put these three low-central vowels in the environment /l.........t/ we could produce the three words ...., ..., and ....

lot   light   lout

254. We will consider one final vowel sound. Pronounce the words *oil*, *join*, and *boy*. They contain a complex vowel. We will represent the first part of this complex with /ɔ/. Is the last part of the complex vowel in *boy* more like the last part of the vowel in *buy* or *bough*?

....

buy

255. The transcription of the vowel in *buy* is / /.

/ay/

256. The complete transcription of *boy* is /bɔ........./.

/bɔy/

257. What words are these?

a) coil   c) coy
b) toil   d) noise

a) /kɔyl/ ....   c) /kɔy/ ....
b) /tɔyl/ ....   d) /nɔyz/ ....

258. The following list contains one example of each of the complex vowels you have studied. Identify the vowel nucleus in each word:

a) /ay/   e) /aw/
b) /ey/   f) /ow/
c) /iy/   g) /uw/
d) /ɔy/

a) buy /   /   e) now /   /
b) bay /   /   f) no /   /
c) bee /   /   g) new /   /
d) boy /   /

259. The first sound in the words *yes*, *yet*, and *use* can be symbolized with /y/. Transcribe these words:

a) /yes/   b) /yet/   c) /yuwz/

a) /   /   b) /   /   c) /   /

260. Since /y/ is used both as part of vowel nuclei and as a consonant, we can refer to /y/ either as a **semi** .... or as a **semi** ....

vowel   consonant

261. The first sound in the words *wet*, *win*, and *wail* can be symbolized with /w/. Transcribe these words:

a) /   /   c) /   /

b) /   /

a) /wet/   c) /weyl/

b) /win/

262. /w/, like /y/, is used both as part of vowel nuclei and as a consonant. We can refer to /w/ either as a .... or a ....

semivowel
semiconsonant

263. As part of a vowel nucleus, /w/ and /y/ represent the movement of the tongue during the pronunciation of the vowel. One of these symbols represents a movement of the tongue toward the high-front position, and the other a movement of the tongue toward the high-back position. Pronounce *buy* (/bay/) and *bough* (/baw/). /-y/ represents movement to the high-............................ position. /-w/ represents movement to the high-............................ position.

front
back

264. Now let's turn to the initial sound in words like *he*, *hat*, *who*, and *hot*. We symbolize this sound as /h/. How would you describe the position of your lips as you pronounce /h/ in /hiy/ *he* and /h/ in /huw/ *who*?

The lips are spread while pronouncing /h/ in *he*, but rounded in *who*.

265. The description of the articulation of /h/ can be done in terms of the vowel that follows. That is, the position of the lips and tongue for the pronunciation of English /h/ is determined by the following vowel. In the pronunciation of /h/ in /hæt/, are the lips rounded or unrounded? ....

unrounded

266. The major difference then between /h/ and a following vowel is that the vowels are voiced, whereas /h/ is ....

voiceless

267. What words are these?

a) is	j) hat	a) /iz/	j) /hæt/ ....
b) his	k) it	b) /hiz/	k) /it/ ....
c) eat	l) hit	c) /iyt/	l) /hit/ ....
d) heat	m) hung	d) /hiyt/	m) /həŋ/ ....
e) ate, eight	n) hope	e) /eyt/	n) /howp/ ....
f) hate	o) whom	f) /heyt/	o) /huwm/ ....
g) edge	p) height	g) /eǰ/	p) /hayt/ ....
h) hedge	q) how	h) /heǰ/	q) /haw/ ....
i) at		i) /æt/	

/pil/   /spil/

268. The /p/ of /pil/ is slightly different from the /p/ of /spil/. For one word the air is released with a puff of air called **aspiration**. Hold your open hand several inches in front of your mouth as you say /pil–spil/ aloud several times. The puff of air is evident for the /p/ of /   /, but not for the /p/ of /   /.

(un)aspirated

269. The /p/ of /pil/ is aspirated, whereas the /p/ of /spil/ is un.......... .

aspirated   (un)aspirated

270. The /k/ of /kil/ and the /k/ of /skil/ are different in the same way that the /p/ sounds of /pil/ and /spil/ are different. In the words /kil/ and /skil/, one /k/ is .... and one is un.......... .

/kil/
/skil/

271. The /k/ of /   / is aspirated.
The /k/ of /   / is unaspirated.

/t/

272. /p/ and /k/ are voiceless stops. The third voiceless stop of English is /   /.

yes

273. Is the /t/ of /til/ different in aspiration from the /t/ of /stil/? ....

The /t/ of /til/ is aspirated but the /t/ of /stil/ is unaspirated.

274. Describe the difference between the /t/ of /til/ and the /t/ of /stil/.

....
....
....

275. So far we have considered the aspiration of the voice-less stops in initial position followed only by the vowel /i/. What happens to the aspiration of initial /p/, /k/, and /t/ when followed by other vowels? Pronounce these words and see.

peel	keel	tail
pole	call	tell
Paul	cull	tile
pal	coal	tall
pale/pail	cool	tool
pool	coil	toll
pull		toil
pile		

We can now make a generalization about the aspiration of the voiceless stops in initial position; namely, when a voiceless stop occurs initially in a word it is

aspirated   ....

SUMMARY OF FRAMES 247–275

Completing our study of vowels are the three complex phonemes:

/ay/, as in *mice*,

/aw/, as in *mouse*, and

/ɔy/, as in *boy*.

When /-y/ and /-w/ are part of complex vowel phonemes, we regard them as semivowels. As part of vowel nuclei, /-y/ and /-w/ represent the movement of the tongue in a higher and more forward direction (/-y/) or in a higher and more backward direction (/-w/) during the articulation of a vowel. But /y/ and /w/ can also be regarded as semiconsonants; they are consonant phonemes as the initial sounds of *yet* and *wet*.

When /h/ is articulated, the mouth assumes the position of the vowel that follows it. Aspiration is a slight puff of air that accompanies voiceless stops in initial position.

Now turn to the vowel chart on page 62 and complete items 12, 13, and 14 and compare your answers with those on page 62.

In this elementary analysis of English phonology you have studied most of the consonant and vowel *sounds* that are used in speaking. In more advanced studies you can also consider other aspects of pronunciation, for example, the use of pitch to distinguish such sentences as *He's a doctor.* from *He's a doctor?* We could also consider the degrees of stress that differentiate *object* in the sentences *I objéct* and

I have an óbject. These and other features of pronunciation that have not been developed in this book can be profitably studied in the following texts:

Buchanan, Cynthia D., *A Programmed Introduction to Linguistics*. Boston: D. C. Heath & Company, 1963.

Gleason, H. A., Jr., *An Introduction to Descriptive Linguistics*, rev. ed. New York: Holt, Rinehart and Winston, Inc., 1961, pp. 14–50.

Hockett, C. F., *A Course in Modern Linguistics*. New York: The Macmillan Company, 1958, pp. 15–61.

King, Harold V., *Guide and Workbook in the Structure of English*. Englewood Cliffs, N.J.: Prentice-Hall, Inc., 1966, pp. 49–76.

Pike, K. L., *The Intonation of American English*. Ann Arbor: University of Michigan Press, 1945.

Prator, Clifford H., Jr., *Manual of American English Pronunciation*, rev. ed. New York: Holt, Rinehart and Winston, Inc., 1957.

With the knowledge you now have of the sound system of English, you are ready to proceed to a study of English grammar in Part Two.

CONSONANT CHART

	Bilabial	Labiodental	Interdental	Alveolar	Alveopalatal	Velar
Stop						
voiceless	1) / /			2) / /		3) / /
voiced	4) / /			5) / /		6) / /
Fricative						
voiceless		7) / /	8) / /	9) / /	16) / /	
voiced		10) / /	11) / /	12) / /	17) / /	
Nasal	13) / /			14) / /		15) / /
Affricate						
voiceless					18) / /	
voiced					19) / /	
Lateral				20) / /		
Retroflex				21) / /		

VOWEL CHART

	Front	Central	Back
high	1) / / /d..........d/ .... 2) / / /d..........d/		10) / / /p..........l/ .... 9) / / /p..........l/ ....
mid	3) / / /br..........d/ .... 4) / / /br..........d/	11) / / /k..........t/	8) / / /p..........l/ ....
low	5) / / /k..........t/	12) / / /f..........nd/ .... 13) / / /f..........nd/ .... 6) / / /k..........t/	14) / / /v..........s/ .... 7) / / /k..........t/ ....

Answers to Consonant Chart

1) /p/	8) /θ/	15) /ŋ/
2) /t/	9) /s/	16) /š/
3) /k/	10) /v/	17) /ž/
4) /b/	11) /ð/	18) /č/
5) /d/	12) /z/	19) /ǰ/
6) /g/	13) /m/	20) /l/
7) /f/	14) /n/	21) /r/

Answers to Vowel Chart

1) /iy/	/diyd/	*deed*		8) /ow/	/powl/	*pole*
2) /i/	/did/	*did*		9) /u/	/pul/	*pull*
3) /ey/	/breyd/	*braid*		10) /uw/	/puwl/	*pool*
4) /e/	/bred/	*bread* or *bred*		11) /ə/	/kət/	*cut*
5) /æ/	/kæt/	*cat*		12) /ay/	/faynd/	*find*
6) /a/	/kat/	*cot*		13) /aw/	/fawnd/	*found*
7) /ɔ/	/kɔt/	*caught*		14) /ɔy/	/vɔys/	*voice*

What do we mean by grammar of English words? Are there rules for the formation of words, as there are for the formation of sentences? Let's take a look at the word *inactivated*. It seems to be made up of a number of parts including *act*, *-ive*, *-ate*, *-ed*, and *in-*. If we were given these elements in random order and were asked to put them together to form a word, would any possible arrangement other than *inactivated* make sense? For example, *ateivinacted* or *actinediveate*? No. The formation of English words follows regular rules, which can be described. Say these two verb forms out loud: *laughed*, *loved*. Both of them end with the written form *-ed*. Is *-ed* pronounced the same in each word? No, *-ed* is pronounced several different ways when it means something like *past*. How it is pronounced with different verbs is regularly predictable once we know the rules. In the pages that follow, we will consider some of the fundamental aspects of word formation in spoken English.

THE GRAMMAR OF ENGLISH WORDS

In this section you will study regular and irregular ways of indicating plurality in nouns. By the end of this section you will be able to:

a) state the three regular ways of indicating plurality;
b) choose—in transcription—the correct Plur sign for regular nouns;
c) define *regular* and *irregular* with respect to nouns;
d) recognize and describe irregular types of pluralization in words;
e) read and write formulas for words including Plur.

SECTION 1

1.
$$\text{The} \left\{ \begin{array}{l} \text{horses} \\ \text{sheep} \\ \text{cows} \\ \text{oxen} \\ \text{goats} \\ \text{lambs} \end{array} \right\} \text{are in the meadow.}$$

All the nouns enclosed in braces in the above example include plurality, the notion of *more than one*; that is, each noun above is the form *noun + plural*. We use the symbol **Plur** for the information that *more than one* has been added in each case. Thus:

a) horse + Plur

b) sheep + Plur

c) cow + Plur

d) ox + Plur

e) goat + Plur

f) lamb + Plur

a) horse + Plur ⟶ horses

b) sheep + Plur ⟶ sheep

c) .... + ... ⟶ cows

d) .... + ... ⟶ oxen

e) .... + ... ⟶ goats

f) .... + ... ⟶ lambs

2. **Affix** is the term for a grammatical element (like the notion *more than one*) that is added to a **base**. In the form *horses*, Plur is an .... added to the

affix

base

affix   base

................., *horse*. In the form *oxen*, Plur is an .... added to the ...., *ox*.

3. Circle the words below that contain an affix.

All are circled.

teachers   children   women

4. The affix contained in the circled words of the preceding frame is the .... affix.

Plur

more than
one

base

sheep

no

/-əz/	/-s/	/-s/
/-z/	/-əz/	/-z/

/-s/
/-z/ and /-əz/

yes

/-əz/

5. Plur represents the notion ....
....

6. An affix is a grammatical element that is added to a
....

7. Usually when Plur is added to a noun there is some
manifestation of its presence. The -s in the spelling of
horses shows that Plur has been added. The -s in the
spelling of *cows* shows the presence of Plur. But it is
clear from the plural noun form .... in
the list of Frame 1 that Plur is not always signaled by
a change in the spelling or pronunciation of the base.

8. Most nouns in English follow a regular pattern of
pluralization. All the following nouns contain Plur,
and in each one the presence of Plur is signaled in a
regular way.

bus*es*	tulip*s*	bandit*s*
violin*s*	peach*es*	bed*s*

Notice that the regular sign of Plur is not always
spelled the same way. Is it always pronounced the same
way? .... Transcribe the plural affixes of the
above six words to find out.

/. /		/ /		/ /	
/ /		/ /		/ /	

9. The three regular indications of Plur are /   /,
/   /, and /   /.

10. Is the Plur sign pronounced the same way in these six
words?

glasses	churches	ashes
phrases	edges	garages

....

11. The sign of Plur that is added to *glass, phrase, church,
edge, ash,* and *garage* is pronounced /   /.

66

12. It is possible to make a generalization about the distribution of the Plur sign /-əz/. Each of the six sample words in the last frame ends with a different sound:

> glass   phrase   church   edge   ash
> garage (if pronounced /gəraž/)

We can now move from these six words to this generalization: When a noun is pluralized in the regular way, the Plur sign /-əz/ is added to a word that ends with any of the six sounds / /, / /, / /, / /, / /, or / /.

/s/ /z/ /č/
/ǰ/ /š/ or /ž/

13. We can hereafter refer to the six sounds /s/, /z/, /š/, /ž/, /č/, and /ǰ/ as **sibilants**. The Plur sign /-əz/ is added to any regular noun ending with a ....

sibilant

14. The sibilants conveniently fall into three voiced/voiceless pairs: / / and /z/, / / and /ž/, and / / and /ǰ/.

/s/   /š/
/č/

15. We found that the choice of the Plur sign /-əz/ was determined by the last sound of the word being pluralized. Similarly, the choice of the voiceless regular Plur signal /-s/, or the voiced regular signal /-z/, is determined by the last sound of the word being pluralized. Add /-s/ or /-z/, whichever is appropriate, to the following words:

/-s/ /-s/ /-s/ /-s/
/-z/ /-z/ /-z/ /-z/
/-z/ /-z/ /-z/

> /map......../   /bet........./   /pik........./   /weyf......./
> /mab......../   /bed........./   /pig........./   /weyv......./
> /teyl......./   /kar........./   /biy......./

16. Which Plur sign (voiced or voiceless) did you add to the words ending in /p/, /t/, /k/, and /f/ above?

....

Did you add the voiced or the voiceless signal to the words ending in /b/, /d/, /g/, /v/, /l/, /r/, and /iy/?

....

voiceless

voiced

Pronounce the first group of phonemes (/p/, /t/, /k/, /f/). Besides the fact that all these are oral sounds, what one feature do they have in common?

....

They are all voiceless.

They are all voiced.

voiced
/z/

voiceless
/s/

/əz/

/z/   /ž/   /ǰ/

/s/   /z/   /š/   /ž/
/č/   /ǰ/ (in any order)

/-z/   Nasals are voiced.

/-z/   The final sounds (/ə/
and /iy/) are voiced.

/-s/
/-z/   /-əz/

What one feature do the phonemes in the second group (/b/, /d/, /g/, /v/, /l/, /r/, /iy/) share?

....

17. The addition of the affix Plur to nouns ending with voiced sounds (other than /z/, /ž/, and /ǰ/) is regularly indicated by the addition of the .... (*voiced* or *voiceless*) phoneme /   /.

18. The addition of Plur to nouns ending with voiceless sounds (other than /s/, /š/, and /č/) is regularly indicated by the addition of the .... (*voiced* or *voiceless*) phoneme /   /.

19. The addition of Plur to nouns ending with sibilants is regularly indicated by the addition of /   /.

20. The sibilants are /s/, /   /, /š/, /   /, /č/, and /   /.

21. All the following nonsense words include the /-əz/ sign of Plur. Complete each word by adding one of the six possible sibilants.

    /skre........əz/   /skre........əz/   /skre........əz/
    /skre........əz/   /skre........əz/   /skre........əz/

22. Which of the three regular signs of Plur would you add to a noun ending with a nasal (e.g., *tone*, *song*, *chime*)? /   / Why? ....

23. Which regular sign of Plur would you add to *sofa* and *city*? /   / Why? ....

....

24. Plur is regularly indicated by the addition of /   /, /   /, or /   / to a base.

25. Suppose the following nouns entered our language from some other language. How would you pluralize them? How would you talk about two of these things?

68

a) /s/

b) /z/

c) /əz/

d) /s/

e) /z/

f) /əz/

g) /z/

h) /əz/

a) one /ðeŋk/   two /ðeŋk......../

b) one /weyŋ/   two /weyŋ......../

c) one /pliynč/   two /pliynč......../

d) one /guwt/   two /guwt......../

e) one /krin/   two /krin......../

f) one /dowǰ/   two /dowǰ......../

g) one /spliy/   two /spliy......../

h) one /tuws/   two /tuws......../

26. A noun is *regular* if the presence of the affix Plur is indicated by the addition of

a sibilant

a voiced sound

/z/   /ž/   /ǰ/

a voiceless sound

/s/   /š/   /č/

/-əz/ to a base ending with .... ,

/-z/ to a base ending with ....

(except /   /, /   /, and /   /),

/-s/ to a base ending with ....

(except /   /, /   /, and /   /).

27. You are aware that some English nouns show the addition of Plur in ways other than by adding /-əz/, /-s/, or /-z/ to a base. A noun that indicates Plur in any way other than by the simple addition of /-əz/, /-z/, or /-s/ is called **irregular**. *Ox*, *sheep*, and *child* are

irregular

.... nouns.

28. Circle the irregular nouns in the list.

mouse

house

path

knife

cat	house	class
mouse	crowd	school
clerk	teacher	path
day	knife	bee

29. Some irregular nouns, like *deer* and *sheep*, have the same form in the singular and the plural. When we add Plur to *deer* and *sheep*, we do not change the pronunciation of the word in any way. The notion *more than one* (Plur) is present, but there is no overt sign of Plur in the word. We speak of this lack of change in form as the addition of a **zero** (written ∅). The change of *deer* from singular to plural involves a

69

change in meaning, but no corresponding change in form.

a) ∅

b) ∅

a) deer + ... ⟶ deer

b) sheep + ... ⟶ sheep

30. Another irregular way of signaling Plur consists of a vowel change. The indication of Plur added to *man* involves a vowel change; the /æ/ of the singular form changes to the vowel /____/ in the plural form.

/e/

31. What is the vowel change in the following nouns when they are pluralized?

	singular		plural
EXAMPLE: *man*	/æ/	changes to	/e/

	singular		plural
a) foot	/ /	changes to	/ /
b) goose	/ /	changes to	/ /
c) mouse	/ /	changes to	/ /

a) /u/   /iy/

b) /uw/   /iy/

c) /aw/   /ay/

32. Some irregular nouns involve two changes when Plur is added. Transcribe the singular and plural forms of the nouns below and tell what two changes occur when each noun is pluralized. (The example is done for you.)

	singular	plural
EXAMPLE: knife	/nayf/	/nayvz/

/f/ changes to /v/; /-z/ is added.

	singular		plural
a) leaf	/	/ /	/
	/	/ changes to / /;	
	/	/ is added.	
b) house	/	/ /	/
	/	/ changes to / /;	
	/	/ is added.	
c) path	/	/ /	/
	/	/ changes to / /;	
	/	/ is added.	

a) /liyf/   /liyvz/

   /f/   /v/

   /-z/

b) /haws/   /hawzəz/

   /s/   /z/

   /-əz/

c) /pæθ/   /pæðz/

   /θ/   /ð/

   /-z/

33. When you pluralized *knife*, *leaf*, *house*, and *path* you did two things to the singular form: (1) you changed

70

yes

/-əz/ after /z/ and /-z/ after
voiced /v/ and /ð/.

the final consonant and (2) you added /-z/ or /-əz/.
After the final consonant was changed, did the selec-
tion of /-z/ or /-əz/ follow the regular pattern of
English pluralization? .... Explain.

....

....

....

34. There are more irregular ways of indicating Plur than
we have accounted for here. However, there are only
three regular ways of signaling the presence of Plur.
What are they and when is each one used?

1) /-əz/ after the sibilants
   (/s, z, š, ž, č, ǰ/)
2) /-z/ after all other
   voiced sounds
3) /-s/ after all other
   voiceless sounds

1) ....

....

2) ....

....

3) ....

....

35. The base *cat* plus the affix Plur results in the form *cats*.

   EXAMPLE: *cat* + Plur ⟶ *cats*.

   Do these:

a) houses
b) roses
c) teeth
d) mice
e) sheep
f) songs
g) phenomena
h) criteria

a) house + Plur ⟶ ....
b) rose + Plur ⟶ ....
c) tooth + Plur ⟶ ....
d) mouse + Plur ⟶ ....
e) sheep + Plur ⟶ ....
f) song + Plur ⟶ ....
g) phenomenon + Plur ⟶ ....
h) criterion + Plur ⟶ ....

the addition of /-əz/, /-z/,
or /-s/ to the base

36. A regular noun is one which indicates Plur by ....

....

SUMMARY OF FRAMES 1–36

The affix Plur—*more than one*—is regularly indicated by adding

   a) /-əz/ to a base ending with one of the sibilants (/s, z, š, ž, č, ǰ/);
   b) /-z/ to a base ending with a voiced sound other than /z, ž, ǰ/;
   c) /-s/ to a base ending with a voiceless sound other than /s, š, č/.

71

A noun that indicates Plur only by adding /-əz/, /-z/, or /-s/ to the base is a *regular* noun. A noun that indicates Plur in any other way is an *irregular* noun. There are many irregular ways to signal the presence of Plur, some involving no change in the base form (∅—zero—as in *deer*, *deer*), some involving a vowel change (*man*, *men*), and some involving a consonant change plus the addition of a regular Plur sign (*wife*, *wives*).

Now turn to the affix chart on page 102. Complete row one by giving the symbol of the noun affix you have just studied and its three regular pronunciations. Check your answers with those on page 102 and then go on to Section 2.

In this section you will study two more English affixes. By the end of this section you will be able to:

a) list, the three regular signs of the possessive and third person singular affixes, and to state the distribution of each;

b) choose—in transcription—the correct Pos and 3PS signals for regular verbs;

c) recognize transcribed words in which the incorrect indication of Pos has been chosen;

d) read and write formulas for words including Pos and 3PS;

e) list the four English verbs that are irregular in their verb + 3PS forms and precisely describe the irregularity for each.

SECTION 2

---

37. A second affix we use in English is the one added to *cat* in the phrase /ðə kæts teyl/ and to *Susan* in /suzənz smayl/. In these phrases we do not mean more than one cat or more than one Susan. This affix does not add the notion *more than one* to the base; it adds the

possession

notion of .... (your own words).

38. We call the affix of possession **Pos**.

Pos

Pos

cat + ... ⟶ cat's

Susan + ... ⟶ Susan's

39. Other examples of the affix Pos are listed below. For each word listed, transcribe the sign of Pos:

EXAMPLE: Lee's /z/

a) /s/   e) /əz/

b) /z/   f) /z/

c) /əz/   g) /s/

d) /z/   h) /əz/

a) Bart's /	/	e) Rose's /	/
b) Bill's /	/	f) dog's /	/
c) Liz's /	/	g) cat's /	/
d) Bard's /	/	h) fish's /	/

How many different pronunciations of the Pos signal

three

are in this list? .... What are they?

/s/   /z/   /əz/

---

40. The presence of the affix Pos, like the presence of the affix Plur, is regularly indicated by adding /-əz/, /-z/, or /-s/ to the base. The choice of which to add to a

73

noun is determined by the final sound of the word. In other words, we choose the appropriate Pos sign in exactly the same way that we choose the appropriate Plur sign—according to the last sound of the base to which it is added.

We add the Pos signal /-əz/ if the base ends with one of the .... : / /, / /, / /, / /, / /, and / /.
We add the Pos signal /-s/ if the base ends with

....

....

We add the Pos signal /-z/ if the base ends with

....

....

sibilants /s/, /z/, /č/, /ǰ/, /š/, /ž/

a voiceless sound other than /s/, /č/, /š/

a voiced sound other than /z/, /ǰ/, /ž/

41. Keeping in mind the rules you have just completed, read the following transcriptions aloud. Then circle those that are INCORRECTLY transcribed.

a) judge's	/ǰəǰs/		f) clock's	/klaks/
b) pig's	/pigz/		g) lady's	/leydiyz/
c) boy's	/bɔyz/		h) child's	/čayldz/
d) church's	/čərčz/		i) wife's	/wayfz/
e) class's	/klæsəz/		j) king's	/kiŋs/

a) /ǰəǰəz/
d) /čərčəz/
i) /wayfs/
j) /kiŋz/

42. To *judge* we add the Pos sign / / since the base ends in / /. To *church* we add the Pos sign / / since the base ends in / /. To *wife* we add the Pos sign / / since the base ends in / /. To *king* we add the Pos sign / / since the base ends in / /.

/-əz/
/ǰ/ /-əz/
/č/
/-s/ /f/
/-z/
/ŋ/

43. The word *lamps* can be described as *lamp* + Plur. *Child's* can be described as *child* + Pos. Describe the following nouns in this way.

a) friend + Pos
b) bridge + Plur
c) leaf + Plur
d) lady + Pos
e) leaf + Pos

a) friend's ....
b) bridges ....
c) leaves ....
d) lady's ....
e) leaf's ....

74

44. Give the resultant form for:

a) women
b) woman's
c) knights
d) knight's
e) sheep
f) sheep's

a) woman + Plur ....
b) woman + Pos ....
c) knight + Plur ....
d) knight + Pos ....
e) sheep + Plur ....
f) sheep + Pos ....

45. We often add both Plur and Pos to a given noun; for example, *child* + Plur + Pos gives *children's*. Add Plur and Pos to the nouns below and write the resulting form.

a) men's
b) presidents'
c) boys'
d) deer's
e) women's

a) man + Plur + Pos ⟶ ....
b) president + Plur + Pos ⟶ ....
c) boy + Plur + Pos ⟶ ....
d) deer + Plur + Pos ⟶ ....
e) woman + Plur + Pos ⟶ ....

46. Complete the following with Plur, Pos, or Plur + Pos.

a) Plur + Pos
b) Plur
c) Pos
d) Plur + Pos
e) Plur
f) Pos

a) boy + ... ⟶ boys'
b) cow + ... ⟶ cows
c) baker + ... ⟶ baker's
d) woman + ... ⟶ women's
e) manager + ... ⟶ managers
f) class + ... ⟶ class's

47. For each regular noun listed below, give the written forms and the transcriptions.

	Spelling	Transcription
EXAMPLE:		
cat + Plur	cats	/kæts/
cat + Pos	cat's	/kæts/
cat + Plur + Pos	cats'	/kæts/

a) crowds   /krawdz/
   crowd's   /krawdz/
   crowds'   /krawdz/

a) crowd + Plur .... / ... /
   crowd + Pos .... / ... /
   crowd + Plur + Pos .... / ... /

b) clerks   /klərks/
   clerk's   /klərks/
   clerks'   /klərks/

b) clerk + Plur .... / ... /
   clerk + Pos .... / ... /
   clerk + Plur + Pos .... / ... /

c) cows   /kawz/
   cow's   /kawz/
   cows'   /kawz/

c) cow + Plur .... / ... /
   cow + Pos .... / ... /
   cow + Plur + Pos .... / ... /

48. For regular nouns, the three forms, noun + Plur, noun + Pos, and noun + Plur + Pos, are *pronounced* .... (*the same* or *differently*). For regular nouns, the forms, noun + Plur, noun + Pos, and noun + Plur + Pos, are *written* .... (*the same* or *differently*).

the same

differently

49. For irregular nouns, however, noun + Plur, noun + Pos, and noun + Plur + Pos are often not pronounced the same way. For example:

a) /šiyps/ can refer to either *sheep* + ...
   or to *sheep* + ... + ...

b) /čildrənz/ refers only to *child* + ...
   + ...

c) /liyvz/ refers to either *leaf* + ... or
   to *leaf* + ... + ...

a) Pos

   Plur + Pos

b) Plur +
   Pos

c) Plur

   Plur + Pos

50. Although represented differently in writing, for regular nouns, the three forms, noun + ... , noun + ... , and noun + ... + ... , are all pronounced the same.

Plur

Pos   Plur

Pos

51. Notice that the Pos form of proper names ending in /z/ often has two equally common pronunciations. *The car that belongs to the Jones family* is either the /jownz kar/ or the /jownzəz kar/; the book that belongs to Charles is either /.................................... buk/ or /.................................... buk/.

/čarlz/

/čarlzəz/

52. The rule for choosing the proper sign of Plur and Pos (/-s/, /-z/, or /-əz/) will help us again with a third English affix. Read the following sentences. In each one, the sign of a third English affix is italicized. Exaggerate the pronunciation of each italicized affix signal and then transcribe it.

a) X walk*s* /   / to work every Monday morning.

b) X run*s* /   / to work every Monday morning.

a) /-s/

b) /-z/

76

c) /-əz/

d) /-s/

e) /-əz/

f) /-z/

g) /-s/

h) /-z/

verbs

c) X march*es* /   / to work every Monday morning.

d) X slink*s* /   / to work every Monday morning.

e) X pranc*es* /   / to work every Monday morning.

f) X drag*s* /   / to work every .Monday morning.

g) X limp*s* /   / to work every Monday morning.

h) X stagger*s* /   / to work every Monday morning.

53. We signal the presence of Plur or Pos by adding /-s/, /-z/, or /-əz/ to nouns. But in the last frame we found that another set of affix signs—also pronounced /-s/, /-z/, and /-əz/—are added to ....

54. Here are the sentences from Frame 52:

$$
X \left\{ \begin{array}{l} \text{walks} \\ \text{runs} \\ \text{marches} \\ \text{slinks} \\ \text{prances} \\ \text{drags} \\ \text{limps} \\ \text{staggers} \end{array} \right\} \quad \begin{array}{l} \text{to work every Monday} \\ \text{morning.} \end{array}
$$

Of the following possible subjects, put those that could substitute for X under A and those that could not under B:

Janet	they
you and Jim	Tom
Mr. Roberts	I
Mr. and Mrs. Roberts	it
the pretty girl	you
we	the horse
he	you and I

77

A
Janet Mr. Roberts the pretty girl he Tom it the horse

B
you and Jim Mr. and Mrs. Roberts we they I you you and I

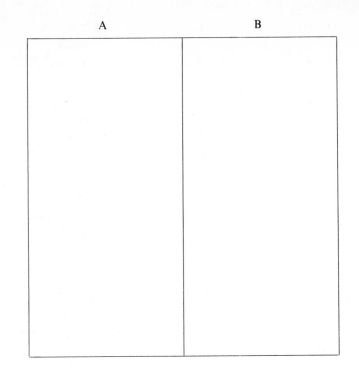

A	B

walk

55. We do say, then, *Janet walks to work every Monday morning*, but not, *you and Jim walks to work every Monday morning*. What form of *walk* do we use if the subject is one of those under B in Frame 54? ....

present

56. *Walks* and *walk*, *runs* and *run*, *marches* and *march*, and so on, are in the .... (*present* or *past*) tense.

57. Look again at the subjects in the A column of Frame 54, the subjects that go with the verb form *walks*.

no   Are any of them plural? ....
no   Are any of them first person (I–we)? ....
no   Are any of them second person (you)? ....
yes   Are they all singular? ....
yes   Are they all third person? ....

third
singular

58. Because this affix sign is added to verbs when the subject is .... (*first* or *second* or *third*) person .... (*singular* or *plural*), we will call it **3PS**.

78

59. Complete the following:

a) runs
b) eats
c) glances

    a) run + 3PS ⟶ ....
    b) eat + 3PS ⟶ ....
    c) glance + 3PS ⟶ ....

60. The 3PS affix is only added to verbs when the verb is

present

third person singular

in the .... tense and when the subject

is ....

If the subject is not third person singular or if the verb
is in the past tense, then 3PS is not added.

61. *Runs*, *eats*, and *glances* exemplify the only three
pronunciations of 3PS. 3PS is always signaled by

/s/   /z/   /əz/

/   /, /   /, or /   /.

62. If the verb base ends with a sibilant, then the 3PS

/əz/

/z/

/s/

signal is pronounced /   /. Otherwise, if the verb
base ends with a voiced sound it is pronounced /   /,
and if it ends with a voiceless sound it is pronounced
/   /.

63. We noticed earlier that the pluralization of certain
nouns is irregular. That is, Plur is not always indicated
by simply adding /-s/, /-z/, or /-əz/ to the base. But
there is only one way to signal 3PS and that is to add
/-s/, /-z/, or /-əz/ to the base. Notice, however, that
when 3PS is present in three English verbs there are
changes within the base.

1) /sez/
2) /dəz/
3) /hæz/

    1) /sey/ *say* + 3PS is pronounced /   /
    2) /duw/ *do* + 3PS is pronounced /   /
    3) /hæv/ *have* + 3PS is pronounced /   /

say

do

have

64. .... (*Say* or *Have* or *Do*) + 3PS involves
a vowel change from /ey/ to /e/. .... (*Say*
or *Have* or *Do*) + 3PS involves a vowel change from
/uw/ to /ə/. .... (*Say* or *Have* or *Do*) +
3PS reflects the loss of the final consonant of the base
before 3PS is added.

79

65. If 3PS were signaled in the regular way in the forms
have + 3PS, *do* + 3PS, and *say* + 3PS, then

/hævz/

have + 3PS would be /   /
(instead of /hæz/)

/duwz/

do + 3PS would be /   /
(instead of /dəz/)

/seyz/

say + 3PS would be /   /
(instead of /sez/)

But *have*, *do*, and *say* are irregular in their verb + 3PS forms.

66. The English verb *be* is irregular in *all* its present tense forms. All other English verbs (even *have*, *do*, and *say*) have only two present tense forms, one form that is used with third person singular subjects, and another form that is used with all other subjects. How many different present tense forms does *be* have? (Look at

three

the sentences below to answer.) ....

I *am* fat.
You (singular) *are* fat.
He/she/it *is* fat.
We *are* fat.
You (plural) *are* fat.
They *are* fat.

is

67. *be* + 3PS is ....

68. The three English verb bases that change form when

say   do

3PS is added are ...., ...,

have

and .... The English verb that is irregular

be

in all its present tense forms is ....

SUMMARY OF FRAMES 37–68

Like Plur, the possessive (Pos) and the third person singular (3PS) affixes are regularly signaled by adding:

1) /-əz/ to a word ending with one of the sibilants;
2) /-z/ to a word ending with a voiced sound other than /z, ž, ǰ/; and
3) /-s/ to a word ending with a voiceless sound other than /s, š, č/.

Pos is added to nouns and 3PS is added to verbs.

It is possible for nouns to include both Plur and Pos as in *the children's toys* or *the boys' campsite*. With regular nouns, the three forms, N + Plur, N + Pos, and N + Plur + Pos, are all pronounced in the same way.

There are four English verbs that change their base when 3PS is present. These are *say*, *have*, and *do*, and also *be*, which is irregular in its other present tense forms as well.

Turn again to the affix chart (page 102) and complete rows two and three with the required information about the two affixes you studied in Section 2. When you have checked your answers (see page 102) begin work on Section 3.

In this section you will study three additional verb affixes and two adjective affixes. By the end of this section you will be able to:

a) list the regular signals of Past and -en and state the distribution of each;

b) choose—in transcription—the correct regular Past and -en signals for verbs;

c) define regular and irregular with respect to verbs and adjectives;

SECTION 3

d) recognize regular and irregular verbs;

e) describe the irregularity present in a given irregular verb;

f) read and write formulas for words including Past, -en, -ing, Cmp, or Sup affixes;

g) identify which affix (from among Plur, Pos, Past, -en, -ing, Cmp, and Sup) a word contains;

h) add the affixes Past, -en, -ing, Cmp, and Sup to bases;

i) specify exactly the difference(s) between a given base noun, verb, or adjective form and its base + affix form (when affix is any one of Plur, Pos, 3PS, Past, -en, -ing, Cmp, or Sup).

---

69. What is the usual meaning of the affix signaled by -*ed* in these words?

walked	waited	waved

past tense

.... (your own words)

70. The verb affix added to *walk*, *wait*, and *wave* in the preceding frame, the affix signaled by the spelling -ed, we will label **Past**.

Past

Past

Past

walk + ... ⟶ walked

wait + ... ⟶ waited

wave + ... ⟶ waved

71. Now transcribe the -ed in the following to determine the different ways you pronounce it.

a) /əd/   g) /d/

b) /t/   h) /əd/

c) /əd/   i) /t/

d) /t/   j) /d/

e) /t/   k) /ɹ/

f) /əd/

a) fad*ed*	/	/	g) liv*ed*	/	/
b) walk*ed*	/	/	h) end*ed*	/	/
c) wait*ed*	/	/	i) stopp*ed*	/	/
d) pass*ed*	/	/	j) drown*ed*	/	/
e) danc*ed*	/	/	k) breath*ed*	/	/
f) part*ed*	/	/			

82

/əd/   /d/   /t/

Past is regularly pronounced in one of three ways. What are they? /   /, /   /, and /   /.

72. The choice from among the three regular Past signals is determined by the final sound of the verb base to which Past is added. The form /-əd/ is added to bases ending in only two different phonemes. Look again at the list of verb + Past words given in Frame 71, then complete the statement below.

/t/ or /d/

The Past sign /-əd/ is only added to verbs ending with /   / or /   /.

73. Transcribe the following list of verbs:

a) /stapt/
b) /pikt/
c) /pæčt/
d) /læft/
e) /pæst/
f) /dæšt/

a) stopped /   /
b) picked /   /
c) patched /   /
d) laughed /   /
e) passed /   /
f) dashed /   /

/t/

voiceless
/t/

In each case, the sign of Past is pronounced /   /. We could make the statement, "The presence of Past is indicated by /t/ when it is added to verb bases ending in /p/, /k/, /č/, /f/, /s/, or /š/." However, an easier and more general statement is possible: The signal of Past is pronounced /t/ when added to verb bases ending with any .... sound except /   /.

74. When to choose the Past sign /-d/ is now a simple matter—we use /-d/ in all cases other than those in which we use /-əd/ or /-t/. In other words, the /-d/ sign of Past is added to verb bases ending with any

voiced   /d/

.... sound except /   /.

/-əd/
/-d/   /-t/

75. Past is regularly indicated by the addition of /-   /, /-   /, or /-   / to a verb base.

83

76. Transcribe the words below, following the example:

EXAMPLE: Past + /tɔk/ *talk* ⟶ /tɔkt/ *talked*

/wɔkt/   Past + /wɔk/ walk ⟶/   /walked
/pleyd/   Past + /pley/ play ⟶/   /played
/wantəd/   Past + /want/ want ⟶/   /wanted
/niydəd/   Past + /niyd/ need ⟶/   /needed

77. When we speak of a noun as regular, we mean that it

/-s/   signals the presence of Plur by adding /   /,
/-z/   /-əz/   /   /, or /   /. And when we refer to a verb as
/-t/   regular, we mean that it signals Past by adding /   /,
/-d/   /-əd/   /   /, or /   / to the base.

78. An irregular verb, on the other hand, is one that signals

in any way other than by   its Past ....

simply adding /-t/, /-d/, ...

or /-əd/   ....

(your own words).

79. There are many irregular verbs. The verbs below are examples of one irregular group. For each verb given, complete the formula.

cut   Past + cut ⟶ ....
hit   Past + hit ⟶..
put   Past + put ⟶ ....
shut   Past + shut ⟶ ....

80. The addition of Past to the verbs above does not result in any change in the pronunciation of the verb. We say that Past is indicated by zero, which we can

∅   symbolize as ....

81. Here's another group of irregular verbs.

bent   Past + bend ⟶ ....
built   Past + build⟶ ....
sent   Past + send ⟶ ....

                     In this irregular class, the addition of Past results in a

/d/   change in the final sound of the verb from /   / to
/t/   /   /.

82. Past added to many verbs results in a change of a vowel: for example, Past + *dig* becomes *dug*. That is, /dig/ becomes /dəg/. Below are additional examples of this type of irregularity. For each one, tell what the vowel change is.

EXAMPLE: dig, win: /i/ changes to /ə/

a) /iy/   /e/   a) bleed, meet, read   /   / changes to /   /
b) /i/   /æ/   b) begin, ring, swim   /   / changes to /   /
c) /ay/   /ow/   c) drive, write, ride   /   / changes to /   /
d) /iy/   /ow/   d) speak, steal   /   / changes to /   /
e) /ay/   /aw/   e) find, wind   /   / changes to /   /
f) /ow/   /uw/   f) blow, know   /   / changes to /   /
g) /e/   /ow/   g) swear, wear   /   / changes to /   /
h) /ey/   /u/   h) shake, take   /   / changes to /   /

83. When Past is added to some verbs, two overt changes occur. What two changes take place when Past is added to these verbs?

creep   feel   mean   sleep   keep

/iy/   /e/   /-t/   /   / changes to /   / and /-   / is added.

84. There is another verb affix whose most common signal is the same as the regular signal of Past, that is, the addition of /-t/, /-d/, or /-əd/ to a verb base. Compare these sentences:

a) John worked.   b) John has worked.

/t/   The -*ed* in both examples is pronounced /   /.

a) John played.   b) John has played.

/d/   The -*ed* in both examples is pronounced /   /.

a) John wanted a car.   b) John has wanted a car.

/əd/   The -*ed* in both examples is pronounced /   /.

a) John needed a rest.   b) John has needed a rest.

/əd/   The -*ed* in both examples is pronounced /   /.

85. All the **a** sentences in the last frame contain examples

Past   of verb + ...

85

86. All the **b** sentences in Frame 84 contain examples of verb + an affix. This affix combined with a verb produces what is called a **past participle**. When the past participle affix is added to the verb base *walk*,

walked

the resulting past participle form is ....

87. In all the **b** examples, the indication of the past participle affix is pronounced / /, / /, or

/t/   /d/
/əd/

/ /, depending on the final sound of the verb base.

88. Compare these sentences:

a) The boy ate the cake.
b) The boy has eaten the cake.

a) The boy broke the record.
b) The boy has broken the record.

a) The boy went home.
b) The boy has gone home.

a) The boy drank the Coke.
b) The boy has drunk the Coke.

a) The boy drove the car.
b) The boy has driven the car.

Again, all the **a** sentences contain examples of

verb	Past

.... + ... ; i.e.,

eat

.... + Past is *ate*;

break

.... + Past is *broke*;

go

.... + Past is *went*;

drink

.... + Past is *drank*; and

drive

.... + Past is *drove*.

89. The verbs in the **a** sentences in the last frame are

simply adding /-t/, /-d/,
or /-əd/

irregular in that Past is not signaled by ....

....

90. Furthermore, we note that the **b** sentences in Frame 88 contain past participles that are neither signaled by the regular addition of /-t/, /-d/, or /-əd/, nor pronounced like the same verbs + Past. That is:

eaten

broken

gone

drunk

driven

past participle + eat $\longrightarrow$ ....

past participle + break $\longrightarrow$ ....

past participle + go $\longrightarrow$ ....

past participle + drink $\longrightarrow$ ....

past participle + drive $\longrightarrow$ ....

91. A regular past participle form is one in which the past participle affix is pronounced /əd/, /d/, or /t/. An irregular past participle form is one in which ....

the past participle is pronounced in any way other than /əd/, /d/, or /t/.

....

....

irregular

92. *Eaten* and *driven* are .... past participles.

93. One common irregular way to indicate the past participle affix is by adding **-en** (pronounced /ən/) to the verb base, as in *eaten*, or by making a change of the vowel in the base and adding -en, as in *driven*. Hereafter we will symbolize the past participle affix as -en no matter how we spell or pronounce its sign. Give the verb + -en form for each of the following and indicate whether it is regular or irregular:

-en + walk $\longrightarrow$	walked	(R)
-en + be $\longrightarrow$	been	(I)
-en + sing $\longrightarrow$		( )
-en + want $\longrightarrow$		( )
-en + take $\longrightarrow$		( )
-en + run $\longrightarrow$		( )
-en + call $\longrightarrow$		( )
-en + bring $\longrightarrow$		( )
-en + love $\longrightarrow$		( )

sung (I)

wanted (R)

taken (I)

run (I)

called (R)

brought (I)

loved (R)

94. A final verb affix to be considered occurs in the following words:

walking   waiting   dancing   cutting

The affix that these verbs have in common is traditionally called the **present participle**. We will simply refer

87

a) going
b) coming
c) singing
d) cutting
e) owing

to it as the **-ing** affix.

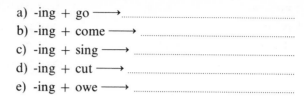

a) -ing + go ⟶ ....
b) -ing + come ⟶ ....
c) -ing + sing ⟶ ....
d) -ing + cut ⟶ ....
e) -ing + owe ⟶ ....

95. The -ing affix is always signaled by adding /-iŋ/ (spelled -ing) to the base form of a verb. Sometimes there are alterations in the spelling of verbs when -ing is added; for example, we double the final *t* of *cut*, and drop the final *e* of *come* and *owe*. But there are no changes in pronunciation:

/kətiŋ/

/kəmiŋ/

/owiŋ/

-ing + cut ⟶   /   /

-ing + come ⟶   /   /

-ing + owe ⟶   /   /

er

96. If John is 6′ 3″ tall and Bill is 6′ 8″ tall we might say that Bill is tall-............ than John.

er

97. Or we might say that John is short-............ than Bill.

(Another affix signaled by -er is added to words like *dance*, *work*, *help*, and *dream*, changing these verbs to nouns meaning *one who dances, one who works*, etc. The other examples of -er—*water*, *father*, and *weather*—do not signal an affix but are simply part of the base.)

98. In the last two frames, you have added the sign of an affix commonly called the **comparative** (Cmp) affix. Circle the words below that contain Cmp. (If in doubt, try putting the word in the sentence "This X is ....-er than that X.")

softer	uglier
warmer	swifter
cheaper	smarter
weaker	

softer	warmer	weather	weaker
father	cheaper	singer	uglier
water	learner	owner	swifter
helper	dancer	dreamer	smarter

Cmp

99. The -er added to *soft* signals the presence of the .... affix. In this case, the relative softness of the two entities is being compared.

adjective	100. The affix Cmp is added to a(n) .... (*adjective* or *noun* or *verb*) base.
	101. Give the Adj (adjective) + Cmp form of the adjectives below:
a) larger	a) large + Cmp ⟶ ....
b) harder	b) hard + Cmp ⟶ ....
c) darker	c) dark + Cmp ⟶ ....
small + Cmp funny + Cmp bright + Cmp	102. .... + ... ⟶ smaller .... + ... ⟶ funnier .... + ... ⟶ brighter
-er	103. Regularly, the Adj + Cmp form is realized as Adj + ...
	104. A second regular way of indicating the presence of Cmp is exemplified in the following sentences. Complete them:
	Susan is beautiful.
more	Susan is .... beautiful than Betty.
	This TV set is expensive.
more	This TV set is .... expensive than that one.
more	Many adjectives are preceded by .... in their Adj + Cmp forms.
	105. But the presence of Cmp can also be signaled in irregular ways. We know that neither *gooder* nor *more good* is the Adj + Cmp form of *good*. *Good* + Cmp
better	⟶ ....
	106. The following words contain an Adj + an affix that is traditionally called the **superlative** affix.

greatest	quickest	coldest
smallest	funniest	warmest

The presence of the superlative affix is usually indicated
-est   by the spelling ....

107. For convenience, we can use the abbreviation Sup for
     the adjective affix called ....

superlative

108. .... + Sup ⟶ greatest

great
small   .... + Sup ⟶ smallest
quick   .... + Sup ⟶ quickest

109. We learned that Cmp has two regular signs. Sup is
     also signaled in a second regular way.

     a) Joan is beautiful.
     b) Joan is more beautiful than Betty.
most c) Joan is the .... beautiful girl I know.

     In sentence **b** above, Adj + Cmp ⟶ more beauti-
     ful. In sentence **c**, Adj + Sup ⟶ ....

most beautiful   ....

110. Many Adj + Sup forms are realized as the word
most .... preceding the adjective base.

111. The change from adjective to Adj + Cmp is regularly
-er   realized either as the addition of .... or as the word
more   .... And the change from adjective to
        Adj + Sup is regularly realized either as the addition
-est   most   of .... or as the word ....

112. Although the choices of -er or *more* to signal Cmp
     and -est or *most* to signal Sup are not completely
     predictable, the -er and -est are usually added to
     words of one or two syllables; *more* and *most* indicate
     Cmp and Sup before longer adjectives.

a) shortest   a) short + Sup ⟶ ....
b) most popular   b) popular + Sup ⟶ ....
c) happiest   c) happy + Sup ⟶ ....
d) most wonderful   d) wonderful + Sup ⟶ ....
e) uglier   e) ugly + Cmp ⟶ ....
f) more difficult   f) difficult + Cmp ⟶ ....
g) sweeter   g) sweet + Cmp ⟶ ....

90

113. There are several irregular Adj + Sup forms—forms that are made in some way other than by

-est

a) the addition of -............... to the adjective base.

most

b) the addition of .... preceding the adjective base.

114. Perhaps the two most frequently occurring irregular Adj + Sup forms are *good* + Sup (which is NOT *goodest* or *most good*) and *bad* + Sup (which is NOT *baddest* or *most bad*). Both *good* + Sup and *bad* + Sup will fit into this sentence:

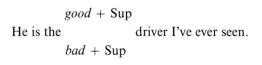

good + Sup
He is the   driver I've ever seen.
bad + Sup

best

good + Sup ⟶ ....

worst

bad + Sup ⟶ ....

115. An adjective is *regular* if (a) it indicates the presence of Cmp by the addition of .... and Sup by

-er

-est

the addition of ...., or (b) it signals the presence of Cmp by the addition of the word

more

.... and Sup by the addition of the word

most

....

116. Plur, Pos, 3PS, Past, -en, -ing, -er, and -est represent the addition of grammatical information (*more than one*, *possession*, etc.) to a base; that is, Plur, Pos, etc.,

affixes

are ....

117. When an affix is added to a base, there is usually some overt sign in the resulting base + affix form that this addition has occurred. The ways of indicating the presence of most affixes can be divided into two

regular

groups: (a) .... (e.g., the addition of /-əz/, /-z/, or /-s/ to signal Pos or the addition of /-əd/, /-d/, or /-t/ to signal Past); or (b)

irregular

.... (e.g., the addition of Ø to signal Plur, or a vowel change to signal Past).

91

118. Following the examples, tell how the affix is indicated in each of the following:

EXAMPLE: foot + Plur   a change of /u/ to /iy/

            boy + Pos   the addition of /z/

a) the addition of /-z/   a) child + Pos

b) the addition of /-z/   b) sailor + Plur

c) the addition of /-əz/   c) sash + Plur

d) the addition of *most*   d) magnificent + Sup

e) the addition of /-s/   e) cat + Plur + Pos

f) the addition of *more*   f) significant + Cmp

g) the addition of /-n/   g) see + -en

h) the addition of /-z/   h) sing + 3PS

i) the addition of -er   i) sticky + Cmp

j) the addition of /-d/   j) try + Past

k) the addition of /-s/   k) think + 3PS

l) the change of /i/ to /ə/   l) swim + -en

m) the addition of -*est*   m) quick + Sup

n) the addition of /iŋ/   n) shake + -ing

o) the addition of ∅   o) hit + Past

119. To review the affixes we have studied so far, complete the following:

a) girls'   a) girl + Plur + Pos ⟶

b) took   b) Past + take ⟶

c) stronger   c) strong + Cmp ⟶

d) does   d) do + 3PS ⟶

e) hit   e) -en + hit ⟶

f) girl's   f) girl + Pos ⟶

g) begun   g) -en + begin ⟶

h) most horrible   h) horrible + Sup ⟶

i) colder   i) cold + Cmp ⟶

j) doing   j) -ing + do ⟶

k) happier   k) happy + Cmp ⟶

l) girls   l) girl + Plur ⟶

m) brightest   m) bright + Sup ⟶

n) seen   n) -en + see ⟶

o) says   o) say + 3PS ⟶

The affix that we symbolize as Past has three regular forms:

1) /əd/ when added to a word ending with /d/ or /t/;
2) /-d/ when added to a word ending with a voiced sound other than /-d/;
3) /-t/ when added to a word ending with a voiceless sound other than /-t/.

A verb is regular if it makes its verb + Past form by simply adding /-əd/, /-d/, or /-t/ as described above. If the verb + Past form is made in any other way, the verb is irregular. There are many irregular ways in which Past is added, including the addition of ∅ (no change: *put*), a vowel change (*began*), a consonant change (*built*), or both a vowel and a consonant change (*felt*).

The -en form (as in *He has walked*) is regularly composed of verb + /-əd/, /-d/, or /-t/ distributed as they are for Past. Again, there are many irregular forms (e.g., *begun, gone, spent*).

The verb affix -ing (as in *walking, singing*) is always pronounced /-iŋ/.

The addition of the grammatical information comparative (Cmp) to an adjective is regularly signaled (1) by the addition of -er to the adjective (*smarter*), or (2) by the addition of *more* before the adjective (*more intelligent*). The addition of superlative (Sup) to an adjective is regularly signaled (1) by the addition of -est to the adjective (*smartest*), or (2) by the addition of *most* before the adjective (*most intelligent*). The distribution of the two regular Cmp and the two regular Sup signals is not entirely predictable, but -er and -est occur most often with one- or two-syllable adjectives, whereas *more* and *most* usually occur with longer adjectives. Irregular Adj + Cmp and Adj + Sup forms occur (e.g., *better, worst*).

Now you are ready to complete the affix chart on page 102. When you have finished rows four to eight and checked your answers (page 102), go on to Section 4.

In this section you will study another class of affixes. By the end of this section you will be able to:

a) define derivational and inflectional affixes in terms of an important general difference between them;

SECTION 4

b) recognize derivational and inflectional affixes in words, and identify them as either derivational or inflectional;

c) determine and state what change in part of speech occurs when derivational affixes are added to particular noun, verb, and adjective bases.

---

120. The affixes we have studied so far are called **inflectional** affixes. When we add inflectional affixes to a base, the new form (base + affix) is usually the same part of speech as the base form was. When we add the inflectional affix Plur to the noun *girl*, the new form (*girls*) is still a noun. When we add the inflectional affix Past to the verb *run*, the new form (*ran*) is still a verb. When we add the inflectional affix Cmp to the adjective *hot*, the new form (*hotter*) is still an adjective. Similarly, if we take any of these inflectional affixes away from the base + affix form, we do not change the part of speech. *Smoothest* is an adjective. *Smooth* is a(n)

adjective
verb
.... *Go* is a verb. *Going* is a(n) ....

121. Plur, Pos, 3PS, Past, -en, -ing, Cmp, Sup are all
inflectional
.... affixes; when they are added to base forms, there is usually no attendant change in the part of speech.

122. However, there is a large set of affixes in English called **derivational** affixes that usually (*not* always) change words from one part of speech to another. Adding the derivational affix signaled by *-al* to the verb base *arrive* we get the noun *arrival*.

COMPARE: They usually *arrive* early.

Their early *arrival* was typical.

The addition of the derivational affix *-ment* to the
verb
.... (*noun* or *verb*) *employ* gives the
noun
.... (*noun* or *verb*) *employment*.

94

COMPARE: They *employ* many new workers each year.

His *employment* was terminated.

123. All the affixes below are derivational. Circle the sign of the affix in every word.

-al	be-	cynical	behead
-able	-ant	laughable	assistant
-ness	-y	kindness	gloomy
-ty		loyalty	

124. The first column below is a list of bases. In the second column, those bases have had affixes added. Indicate whether each affix in the second column is an inflectional or derivational affix by writing either I (inflectional) or D (derivational) beside it.

EXAMPLE: walk   walked   I

friend   friendly   D

a) D	a) beast	beastly	....
b) D	b) pertain	pertinent	....
c) I	c) smooth	smoothest	....
d) I	d) dog	dogs	....
e) D	e) secure	security	....
f) I	f) run (verb)	runs	....
g) D	g) wide	width	....
h) I	h) cheap	cheaper	....
i) D	i) enter	entrance	....

125. Sometimes the addition of a derivational affix changes a noun form to a verb form.

You are my *friend*.
You *befriend* me.

be-
befriend

The addition of the affix .... to the noun *friend* gives the verb .... in the above example.

126. You bring me *joy*.
I *enjoy* your company.

en-   noun
verb

The addition of the affix .... changes the .... (*noun* or *verb*) *joy* to the .... (*noun* or *verb*) *enjoy*.

127. And sometimes the addition of a derivational affix changes a verb form to a noun form.

> You *teach* me.
> You are my *teacher*.

-er   verb
noun

The addition of the affix .... to the .... (*noun* or *verb*) teach gives the .... (*noun* or *verb*) *teacher* in the above example.

128. Following the examples given, complete each sentence below with the verb (italicized) + a noun-making affix.

> EXAMPLE: If you *please* someone, you bring him *pleasure*.

When you *discover* something, you make a

discovery

....

When you *approve* something, you give it your

approval

....

One way to *advertise* something is to make an

advertisement

....

When you *decide* something, you make a

decision

....

If you *assist* someone, you are his

assistant

....

129. Complete the sentences below by writing the correct word in the blank. Then, in the parentheses, write N if the word you have chosen is a noun, or V if the word you have chosen is a verb.

> EXAMPLE: **amuse, amusement:**
> a) You ....amuse........ (V) me.
> b) Your ....amusement........ (N) is embarrassing.

congregate, congregation:

> a) Every night they ....
> (   ) on the corner.

a) congregate (V)
b) congregation (N)

> b) The .... (   )
> sang a hymn.

96

a) Warm (V)

b) warmth (N)

a) siege (N)
b) besiege (V)

a) rage (N)

b) enrage (V)

warm, warmth:

a) .... (   ) yourself by the fire.

b) The .... (   ) of the fire was welcome.

siege, besiege:

a) The..(   ) was a success.

b) Don't .... (   ) me with questions.

rage, enrage:

a) His .... (   ) is uncalled for.

b) You .... (   ) me.

130. Some adjective bases can be made into noun or verb forms by the addition of certain affixes. The adjective base *dark* becomes a noun form when the affix -ness is added (*darkness*); it becomes a verb form when the affix -en is added (*darken*):

The *dark* room frightens him. (A)
The *darkness* of the room frightens him. (N)
Don't *darken* the room; you will frighten him. (V)

In the sentences below, circle each affix signal and indicate whether each italicized word is a noun, verb, or adjective by writing N, V, or A in the parentheses.

V
-ance   N
-able   A
A
-en   V

-ness   N
V
-ive   A
-ion   N

I *accept* your proposal. (   )
The *acceptance* was a surprise. (   )
Your proposal is *acceptable*. (   )
Those tomatoes aren't *ripe* yet. (   )
They will *ripen* if you leave them in the sun. (   )
I can't guarantee the *ripeness* of those tomatoes. (   )
Can't you *act* intelligently? (   )
He is an *active* boy. (   )
His *action* was inexcusable. (   )

131. Some typical noun-making affixes are:

-age   -al   -ure   -ing   -ant   -er   -ness   -ity

Notice that each affix can only be added to certain bases. We can add -age to the base *use* (giving us the

97

word *usage*). But we cannot add the affixes -ure or -ity to *use*; there is no English word *usure*, or *usity*. Add each of the above noun-making suffixes to one of the bases below. Make sure that the resulting word is a noun. Use each suffix only once.

dismissal

failure

brightness

breakage

reality

blessing

dancer

accountant

dismiss ....

fail ....

bright ....

break ....

real ....

bless...

dance..

account ....

132. Likewise, each verb-making affix can be added to only certain bases. Add be-, -en, and en- to the three bases below, changing them into verbs.

bewitch

enslave

soften

witch ....

slave ....

soft ....

133. The derivational affixes that typically change bases into adjective forms are also limited in respect to the particular bases with which they can occur. Add each of the given affixes only once to make adjectives out of the bases listed below.

-y   -ly   -al   -ed   -ent   -able

EXAMPLE: choose + -en ⟶ .... chosen

a) -y   dusty

b) -able readable

c) -ent   inherent

d) -ly   stately

e) -ed   aged

f) -al   national

a) dust + ... ⟶ ....

b) read + ... ⟶ ....

c) inhere + ... ⟶ ....

d) state + ... ⟶ ....

e) age + ... ⟶ ....

f) nation + ... ⟶ ....

134. Earlier (Frame 94) we introduced an inflectional affix, -ing. That affix is added to verbs and is used in

sentences such as, *The boy is talking*. There is another affix -ing. It is derivational, and is also added to verbs, but the resultant word is an adjective. The following sentence could be an example of either verb + -ing (I) or verb + -ing (D).

The boy is revolting.

This sentence could mean (a) that the boy is staging a protest against some authority, or (b) that he is in some way repulsive. In the second interpretation, *revolting* is a case of a verb + a(n) .... (*D or I*) suffix.

D

135.   a) The ladies are entertaining.
        b) Janet is striking.

On reading the first sentence, you may picture a group of prettily dressed ladies pouring tea for guests. Or you may simply think of ladies who are amusing in some way. In the second—is Janet protesting against management or does she have a particularly attractive appearance? In both cases, the verb + -ing form can be understood as either a(n) .... (part of speech) or as a(n) .... (part of speech).

verb

adjective

136. If *entertaining* and *striking* in sentences **a** and **b** of the above frames are understood as verbs, then -ing is a(n) .... affix. If they are understood as adjectives, then -ing is a(n)............................ .... affix.

inflectional

derivational

137. In the following sentences, the verb + -ing forms cause no confusion.

The meeting was held at my home.
The setting made an effective background for the action in his story.

In these cases, the verb + -ing form is clearly a(n) .... This -ing is a(n) .... (*D or I*) affix.

noun   D

99

138. In the parentheses beside each sentence below, write A if the verb + -ing form is an adjective, N if it is a noun, and V if it is a verb. (If it is an A, you could put *very* before it.)

V   The child is sleeping. (   )

V   We're coming. (   )

N   The gathering (   ) was a cheerful one.

A   I think she's stunning (   ), don't you?

V   He's swimming (   ) in the district meet.

V   She's charming (   ) him with her smooth talk.

A   She's a charming (   ) girl.

139. A base + affix form is usually the same part of speech as the base if the affix is a(n) .... **inflectional** affix. A base + affix form is usually a part of speech different from the base if the affix is a(n) .... **derivational** affix.

140. Again, there are exceptions to the general statements about English affixes. There are a few derivational affixes whose addition to a base does not result in a change in the part of speech. The italicized words in the sentences below demonstrate the addition of affixes that do not change the part of speech. Circle the added affixes.

He is *partial* in his judgment.

im- He is *impartial* in his judgment.

That matter is *relevant* to this discussion.

ir- That matter is *irrelevant* to this discussion.

They *gained* admittance to the organization.

re- They *regained* admittance to the organization.

She is very *social* in her dealings with others.

anti- She is very *antisocial* in her dealings with others.

That consideration is *important*.

un- That consideration is *unimportant*.

He is a very *interested* student.

dis- He is a very *disinterested* student.

He *tied* his shoe.

un- He *untied* his shoe.

re- He *retied* his shoe.

The class of inflectional affixes includes Plur, Pos, 3PS, Past, -en, -ing, Cmp, and Sup. When inflectional affixes are added to nouns, verbs, or adjectives, the base + inflectional affix form is the same part of speech as the base form was; for example, *run* (verb + Past ⟶ *ran* (verb). However, the addition of a derivational affix to a base usually results in a change in part of speech; the part of speech of the base form is different from that of the base + derivational affix form; for example, *end* (noun) + -less ⟶ *endless* (adjective); *dance* (verb) + -er ⟶ *dancer* (noun).

There are many derivational affixes, many ways of indicating a part of speech change. But each derivational affix is used in combination with particular nouns, verbs, or adjectives. Unlike the case of the regular forms of the inflectional affixes, Plur, Pos, 3PS, Past, -en, no general statement concerning the distribution of derivational affixes is possible.

Word formation in English is systematic. Particular word elements are chosen, combined, and expressed according to certain rules that the native English speaker knows but cannot verbalize at an early age. Have you ever heard a child who is a native speaker of English say *I sawed* /sɔd/ *him*, or *I runned* /rənd/ *away*? The child who /sɔd/ or /rənd/ has internalized the regular rules for indicating the addition of Past to a base. His "error" is not that he does not know the rules for indicating verb + Past forms, but that he has used his regular rule in exceptional cases where it does not apply. It is highly unlikely that the child would say *I* /sɔt/ *him* or *I* /sɔəd/ *him*, *I* /rənt/ *away* or *I* /rənəd/ *away*, for these would be violations of the system. Similarly, the child might conceivably say *those* /mænz/, but he probably would *not* say *those* /mæns/ or *those* /mænəz/. He knows the system; he does not yet know which particular cases are exceptions to it, or in what respect they are irregular. In Part Two we have turned our attention to the regular patterns of word formation and ways of talking about them, and we have looked at instances of irregularity or deviation from the regular rules.

For purposes of convenience we have divided our study of English into three parts, one part dealing with the sound system, one part with the system of word formation, and one part, Part Three, with the system of sentence formation. However, these divisions must not obscure the vital interdependence that exists between the production of sounds, words, and sentences. In Parts One and Two we saw that words can be described—at one level—as combinations of sounds. We also saw that a consideration of English sounds was crucial to our selection of the appropriate regular sign of Plur, Pos, 3PS, Past, and -en. Clearly, the sound system and the grammar of English words are interdependent. But we also saw how the addition of certain affixes was dependent on other sentence elements. For example, the addition of the affix 3PS to a verb depends on factors outside the word itself; the presence of 3PS depends on the type of subject that is contained in the sentence. And we saw how the addition of derivational affixes usually results in a part of speech that is different from that of the base form. To change a word from one part of speech to another is to change its relationship to other words. The interdependence of word grammar and sentence grammar will continue to be evident in Part Three, which you are now ready to begin. For further study of the grammar of English words see:

Francis, W. Nelson, *The English Language: An Introduction*, New York: W. W. Norton & Company, Inc., 1965, pp. 24–36.

Gleason, H. A., Jr., *An Introduction to Descriptive Linguistics*, rev. ed. New York: Holt, Rinehart & Winston, Inc., 1961, pp. 92–110.

Roberts, Paul, *Modern Grammar*, New York: Harcourt, Brace & World, Inc., 1968.

AFFIX CHART

	Affix Symbol	Regular Signs
Noun	1) .... 2)	/ / / / / / / / / / / /
Verb	3) .... 4) .... 5) .... 6)	/ .... (spelling)
Adjective	7) .... 8)	.... (spelling) .... (spelling) .... (spelling) .... (spelling)

Answers to Affix Chart

1) Plur	/-əz/	/-z/	/-s/	5) -en	/-əd/	/-d/	/-t/
2) Pos	/-əz/	/-z/	/-s/	6) -ing	/iŋ/	-ing	
3) 3PS	/-əz/	/-z/	/-s/	7) Cmp	-er	more	
4) Past	/-əd/	/-d/	/-t/	8) Sup	-est	most	

Consider this question: How is it that you as a speaker of English can understand and produce an endless number of sentences that you have never heard or never spoken before? For example, suppose you were to meet a total stranger who said, "The giraffe carefully observed the ant's progress up the barber pole." Of course, you would immediately understand exactly what had been said. You might wonder about the stranger's sanity, but you would understand. You may say to yourself, "Naturally I would understand because I know what all the words in that sentence mean." But notice that these same words given in a list do not provide the meaning that they do when they are arranged as in the sentence above:

barber pole	up
ant's	the
giraffe	carefully
progress	observed

In fact, read or said in this sequence, the words nearly amount to complete nonsense. Clearly, the knowledge you have of the way in which words are arranged and rearranged in sentences provides much of the meaning that permits you to understand sentences that you have never heard before. As a speaker of English, you have learned to interpret that meaning. Furthermore, you have learned to produce sentences with arrangements of words that are meaningful to other speakers of English. It is this ability to form and interpret sentences that will concern us in this part of the program.

THE GRAMMAR OF ENGLISH SENTENCES

In this section you will become aware of three important kinds of knowledge you already have about the grammar of English sentences. You will study basic sentences and the process of negating them. By the end of this section you will be able to:

a)   identify the basic sentence underlying a derived sentence;

b)   describe two different ways of negating basic sentences, and state the conditions required for the choice of each;

c)   list the modals.

---

1. What do you know about English sentences? As a matter of fact, you know a great deal. Only one of these is a grammatical English sentence:

   a) This is the ring that he found it.
   b) This is the ring that he find.
   c) These is the ring that he found.
   d) This is the ring that he found.
   e) This are the ring that he found.
   f) This is the ring whom he found.

d

Sentence .... is grammatical.

2. As speakers of English, we know that sentence **d** is grammatical—that it is an acceptable arrangement of appropriate English words and word groups. This does not mean that we all know how to talk about acceptable sentence formation in technical terms. The point is that we do know which sentences of our language are correctly formed (grammatical) and which are not correctly formed (ungrammatical). Put G beside the grammatical sentences below and U beside the ungrammatical ones.

   a) All that long hot afternoon I wondered whether or not her would come. ....

a) U

   b) If I had enough money, I'd leave for Rio on the next plane. ....

b) G

   c) No any of the bananas were ripe. ....

c) U

   d) He used to come every day, but now he just comes on Thursdays. ....

d) G

105

e) G

f) U

g) U

e) I'm going to go to class tomorrow, although I'd really rather stay in bed. ....

f) Will you please buy me a walking when you go to the supermarket? ....

g) You wash herself every day, don't you? ....

3. Here's a rather strange looking sentence:

The blugy chinzels slottled prasily on the flubbish wub.

Answer these questions about the nonsense sentence above.

a) What kind of chinzels were they?

a) blugy
....

b) What did the chinzels do?

b) slottled
....

c) Where?

c) on the flubbish wub
....

d) What kind of wub did they slottle on?

d) flubbish
....

e) How did they slottle?

e) prasily
....

4. How is it that you are able to answer nonsense questions about a nonsense sentence with no trouble? The nonsense sentence in the last frame includes many grammatical signals that you as a speaker of English recognize as meaningful. Some of these grammatical signals are affixes: The blug*y* chinzel*s* slott*led* prasi*ly* on the flubb*ish* wub. The affix *-ly* helped you to recognize *prasily* as a word that functions like *slowly*, *quietly*, *anxiously*, *quickly*, etc. The *-y* affix of *blugy* you recognized as an adjective-forming affix as in *foggy*, *pithy*, *messy*, etc. The *-ed* of *slottled* signaled Past, the *-s* of *chinzels* signaled Plural, and *-ish* of *flubbish* signaled an adjective affix as in *bluish*, *boyish*, etc. Underline the five affixes in the following nonsense sentence that help you to understand it:

-'s   -ness   -ity
-ed   -er

The flude's klupness and drupity sprungled the tobbler.

106

5. In addition to the presence of affix signs, you had other clues to the grammatical interpretation of the nonsense sentence of Frame 3. How did you know, for example, that it was the *chinzels* and not the *wub* that did the *slottling*? And how did you know that it was the *wub* (not the *chinzels*) that was *flubbish*? We learned in Part Two that we do not put word elements together in random order when we form words. *Childish* is acceptable; *childly* and *ishchild* are not. *Unpresentable* is all right; *dispresentable* and *able-unpresent* are not all right.

So it is with the formation of English sentences; we don't put just any sentence elements together in random order. You know that the order subject–verb is basic to English; therefore you immediately understood the combination *chinzels slottled* as a subject–verb combination, grammatically parallel to *dogs barked, boys ran, things happened*, etc. Likewise, a noun in English is typically preceded by its modifiers. Knowing this, you interpreted *blugy chinzels* and *flubbish wub* as modifier–noun combinations, grammatically similar to *fat man, howling wind, red cheeks*, etc.

Below are three incomplete sentences, each with one slot or position unfilled. The order of sentence elements is already established. In the list given, circle every word that could fill the slots and make a grammatical sentence.

a) ate
   saw
   wanted
   brought

b) cheese
   cash
   peanuts

c) ill   singing
   beautiful   teachers
   discouraged
   here

a) I _____ an apple.

to	lazy
ate	smaller
saw	Bob
wanted	brought

b) I'd like some _____ .

choose	sleepily
cheese	swim
cash	peanuts
green	prettiest

c) They're _____ .

go	here
ill	singing
beautiful	quickly
discouraged	teachers

107

6. Only certain sentence elements are selected to go with other sentence elements. Further, only certain word arrangements are acceptable in English sentence formation. *He saw the cat* is an acceptable arrangement; *The saw he cat* is not. Give one acceptable arrangement for each scrambled sentence below.

a) cafeteria him Saturday I the in every see

....

....

b) for never class he's late

....

....

c) right couldn't envelopes they find were any the size that

....

....

a) Every Saturday I see him in the cafeteria. [or] I see him in the cafeteria every Saturday. [or] I see him every Saturday in the cafeteria.

b) He's never late for class.

c) They couldn't find any envelopes that were the right size.

7. You know which sentences are grammatical and which are ungrammatical. You know that part of the meaning of an English sentence is signaled by the order of the words, and by the affixes that make up those words. What else do you know about English sentences? You know that certain sentences are ambiguous; that is, some sentences can be interpreted in more than one way. Taken out of context, the sentence *Call me a taxi* can be a request for a hired car or a request for a change of name (*OK, you're a taxi*). If we change the sentence to *Call a taxi for me*, it is no longer ambiguous; now only one interpretation is possible. In the sentence *Tom looked at the girl with a smile*, we aren't sure who is smiling, the *girl* or *Tom*. We can make the sentence unambiguous by changing the structure in several ways, among them:

Smiling, Tom looked at the girl.
Tom looked at the girl who was smiling.
Tom looked at the smiling girl.

For each of the following sentences, at least two different interpretations are possible. Following the example, write two possible interpretations of each.

108

We have more difficult assignments now.
Now we have more assignments that are difficult.
Now we have assignments that are more difficult.

a) That's a handbag belonging to a beautiful woman.

That's a beautiful handbag for a woman.

b) Lions which are hunting can be dangerous.

To hunt lions can be dangerous.

a) That's a beautiful woman's handbag.

....

....

....

....

b) Hunting lions can be dangerous.

....

....

....

....

8. In addition to recognizing English sentences that are grammatical, ungrammatical, ambiguous, and unambiguous, you can also recognize that certain sentences are grammatically related to one another, as demonstrated in the sentences **a** through **k** below:

a) The boy smoked a cigarette behind the barn yesterday.
b) The boy didn't smoke a cigarette behind the barn yesterday.
c) The boy smoked a cigarette behind the barn yesterday, didn't he?
d) The boy didn't smoke a cigarette behind the barn yesterday, did he?
e) Did the boy smoke a cigarette behind the barn yesterday?
f) When did the boy smoke a cigarette behind the barn?
g) Where did the boy smoke a cigarette yesterday?
h) Who smoked a cigarette behind the barn yesterday?
i) What did the boy smoke behind the barn yesterday?
j) What did the boy do behind the barn yesterday?
k) A cigarette was smoked by the boy behind the barn yesterday.

For each of the five italicized sentences below, circle the number (1, 2, or 3) of the sentence that is *grammatically* related to it.

The worm ate the apple.
1) Worms like apples.
2) The apple was eaten by the worm.
3) Nobody likes wormy apples.

2

You'll see him tomorrow.
1) When will you see him?
2) He'll be standing by the fence.
3) He'll have a surprise for you.

1

The teacher was carrying a switch.
1) The teacher was cruel.
2) What was the teacher carrying?
3) Was the teacher angry?

2

The ant climbed a barber pole.
1) Ants are persevering.
2) Barber poles are easy to climb.
3) The ant didn't climb a barber pole, did it?

3

I pay bills on time.
1) Who pays bills on time?
2) Paying bills is a headache.
3) John pays his bills on time, too.

1

9. We can say that sentence **a** of Frame 8 is **basic** to each of the sentences **b** to **k**. That is, all the sentences **b** to **k** can be derived from sentence **a**. If sentence **a**:

The boy smoked a cigarette behind the barn yesterday.

is basic to sentence **b**:

The boy didn't smoke a cigarette behind the barn yesterday.

what is the sentence that is basic to the sentence:

The cat didn't fall down the chimney last night.

The cat fell down the
chimney last night.

....

....

Sentence **a** is also basic to sentence **d**:

a) The boy smoked a cigarette behind the barn yesterday.

d) Did the boy smoke a cigarette behind the barn yesterday?

What is the sentence that is basic to the sentence:

Will Jack deliver the paper here tomorrow?

....

....

Jack will deliver the paper here tomorrow.

Sentence **a** is also basic to sentence **f**:

a) The boy smoked a cigarette behind the barn yesterday.

f) The boy smoked the cigarette behind the barn yesterday, didn't he?

What sentence is basic to the sentence:

The butcher doesn't bring a roast every week, does he?

....

....

The butcher brings a roast every week.

Note that the sentence, *The butcher brings a roast every week*, is basic to the negative sentence, *The butcher doesn't bring a roast every week*, which in turn is related to the sentence, *The butcher doesn't bring a roast every week, does he?*

And sentence **a** is basic to sentence **k**:

a) The boy smoked a cigarette behind the barn yesterday.

k) A cigarette was smoked behind the barn yesterday.

What sentence is basic to the sentence:

Notes were taken in class by students during the lecture.

....

....

The students took notes in class during the lecture.

10. Our basic sentence can be rendered in a more general way as follows:

The boy (someone)	smoked (verb)	a cigarette (something)	behind the barn (someplace)	yesterday (sometime)

Using the more general forms as necessary, complete the following as done in the example.

EXAMPLE:

IF   When did the boy smoke a cigarette behind the barn?

is derived from

The boy smoked a cigarette behind the barn yesterday (= sometime).

THEN   When did the dog find the bone in the hole?

is derived from

The dog found the bone in the hole sometime.

a)

IF   Where did the boy smoke a cigarette yesterday?

is derived from

The boy smoked a cigarette behind the barn (= someplace) yesterday.

THEN   Where did Janet leave the car last night?

is derived from

....

....

Janet left the car someplace last night.

b)

IF   Who smoked a cigarette behind the barn yesterday?

is derived from

The boy (= someone) smoked a cigarette behind the barn yesterday.

THEN   Who smashed the pitcher in the sink last night?

is derived from

....

....

Someone smashed the pitcher in the sink last night.

c)

Paul should bring some-
thing to the party
Saturday.

IF   What did the boy smoke behind the barn
yesterday?

is derived from

The boy smoked a cigarette (= something) behind the barn yesterday.

THEN   What should Paul bring to the party
Saturday?

is derived from

....

....

d)

I can meet you at the club
sometime.

IF   When did the boy smoke a cigarette
behind the barn?

is derived from

The boy smoked a cigarette behind the
barn yesterday (= sometime).

THEN   When can I meet you at the club?

is derived from

....

....

e)

The doctor gave the patient
an injection at home
yesterday.

IF   A cigarette was smoked behind the barn
by the boy yesterday.

is derived from

The boy smoked a cigarette behind the
barn yesterday.

THEN   The patient was given an injection at
home by the doctor yesterday.

is derived from

....

....

11. Sentences **a**, **b**, and **c** in each of the following sets are
derived from a common basic sentence.

    a) The mouse won't find the cheese in the trap
tonight.

    b) Will the mouse find the cheese in the trap
tonight?

    c) What will the mouse find in the trap tonight?

The mouse will find the
cheese in the trap tonight.

The basic sentence is:

....

....

    a) The car was driven to school by Sam.
    b) Sam drove the car to school, didn't he?
    c) Who drove the car to school?

The basic sentence is:

....

....

Sam drove the car to
school.

    a) When did the mailman put the letter in the box?
    b) The letter was put in the box by the mailman this morning.
    c) Where did the mailman put the letter this morning?

The basic sentence is:

....

....

The mailman put the letter
in the box this morning.

12. Your ability to recognize grammatically related sentences is important in understanding the system of sentence formation in English. When we studied the system of word formation in Part Two, we found that it is possible to talk about affixation in terms of the application of a limited number of general rules. If we know the general rules by which nouns are pluralized, we do not have to deal with every instance of pluralization as a special case. The situation is similar with sentence grammar. Again we find that there is a system of regular rules—a framework—by which we can interpret or understand any particular sentence as the result of the application of certain rules; we do not have to treat every sentence as a special case. This greatly simplifies the task of understanding the structure of English sentences.

    When we studied word grammar, it was helpful to describe affixation as an addition to a base, which (addition) was signaled by a change from the base form to the base + affix form. Thus, *friends, befriend, friendly, friendship, friendliest* can all be interpreted as a base form (*friend*) plus those changes required by

114

the addition of a particular affix. And the forms *friends, befriend, friendly,* etc., are all related by virtue of the fact that they contain the same base, *friend.* Relations among sentences can be interpreted in a similar way. The sentences in the set in Frame 8 are all grammatically related in that they all have a common base sentence. They differ from one another to the extent that the processes that have operated on that base differ.

Let's look now at some basic sentences and their related negatives to see how they are related in terms of the application of certain rules to those basic sentences.

The boy may smoke the cigarette.

The negative of this sentence is:

The boy may not smoke the cigarette.

....

....

13. You made the negative sentence by putting the word .... after the word ....

not   may

14. Make this sentence negative:

The boy has smoked the cigarettes.

The boy has not smoked the cigarettes.

....

....

15. You made the sentence in the last frame negative by putting .... after the word .... (which is a form of *have*).

not   has

16. Give the negative of:

The boy is smoking the cigarettes.

The boy is not smoking the cigarettes.

....

....

17. You made the last sentence negative by putting the word .... after the word .... (which is a form of *be*).

not   is

115

18.

The boy may			smoke the cigarettes.
The boy has	}	NOT {	smoked the cigarettes.
The boy is			smoking the cigarettes.

not

may   have

be

From the three sentences we've made negative so far, we might make a rule about the formation of negative sentences: To make a sentence negative, put .... after ...., a form of ...., or a form of ....

19. Reread the rule you formed in the last frame. Can you apply it to make the following sentence negative?

The boys smoke the cigarettes.

no

....

20. The rule cannot be applied in making the above sentence negative because that sentence does not in-

may   have   be

clude ...., ..., or ....

21. Clearly the rule we made for forming negative sentences is not complete. We will have to add to that rule if we want to cover sentences like: *The boys smoke the cigarettes.*

a) The boys smoke the cigarettes.
b) The boys do not smoke the cigarettes.

What two things were done to make the affirmative sentence, **a**, into the negative sentence, **b**?

1) not

2) do

1) Add ....
2) Add ....

22. Each sentence below requires the addition of two words to make it negative. Every one requires the addition of *not*. Study the sentences given to see what other additional word they require.

They came yesterday.
They did not come yesterday.

116

He comes every Tuesday.
He does not come every Tuesday.

We come every Tuesday.
We do not come every Tuesday.

They got all A's.
They did not get all A's.

We get all A's.
We do not get all A's.

John gets all A's.
John does not get all A's.

When made negative, the sentences given require the
addition of *not* and some form of *do*, either

do   does   did

........................., ..., or ....

23. In making basic sentences negative, it is always
    necessary to add *not*. In making some basic sentences
    negative it is also necessary to add *do*. Read each
    sentence below and decide whether it forms its negative
    (1) by simply adding *not*, or (2) by adding *not* and *do*.
    If it forms its negative by simply adding *not*, then
    write the italicized word(s) of that sentence in Column
    I. If it forms its negative by adding *not* and *do*, then
    write the italicized word(s) in Column II as in the
    examples given.

    EXAMPLES: The baby *played* contentedly.
              You *must visit* us tomorrow.
              I *can buy* that hat.

    a) I *shall bring* my notes.
    b) They *plan* to leave next Wednesday.
    c) They *will see* him tomorrow.
    d) He *may arrive* by noon.
    e) She *walks* to school.
    f) He *has gone*.
    g) Don *is running* for class president.
    h) We *sing* in the choir.
    i) I *have eaten*.
    j) You *studied* hard for that test.
    k) You *are forgetting* your manners.
    l) I *am trying*.

117

	I

```
EX. must visit
EX. can buy
a) shall bring
c) will see
d) may arrive
f) has gone
g) is running
i) have eaten
k) are forgetting
l) am trying
```

	II

```
EX. played
b) plan
e) walks
h) sing
j) studied
```

I (*not*)	II (*do + not*)
must visit can buy	played

---

24. Of the phrases in Column I of the last frame, some include *be* and some include *have*. Each remaining phrase includes a **modal**. These modals are

........................, ..., ...,

........................, and ....

can   shall   will
may   must

25. Sentences that are made negative by the simple addition of *not* are those sentences that include a .... (i.e., *can*, *shall*, *will*, *may*, or *must*), ..., or ....

modal
have   be

26. Modals (hereafter M) include *can*, *shall*, ..., *may*, and ....

will
must

27. Sentences that require *do* + not when made negative are all those that include a verb, but *do not* include ...., ..., or ....

M (modal)   have   be

28. *He is leaving soon* is made negative by adding only ...., since it includes a form of ....

not   be

not
have

29. *He has fired his secretary* is made negative by adding only ...., since it includes a form of ....

not
M (may)

30. The sentence *He may come by noon* is made negative by the addition only of ...., since it contains a ....

can
will   may   must
shall

31. The symbol M may represent ...., ..., ..., ..., or ....

SUMMARY OF FRAMES 1–31

In learning about English sentences, you are not starting from scratch. You already recognize sentences as grammatical or ungrammatical, as ambiguous or unambiguous, as related or unrelated to one another. Given an ungrammatical sentence, you can supply its grammatical form. Given an ambiguous sentence, you not only recognize that it is ambiguous, but also know in what way(s) it is ambiguous; you know what its several possible interpretations are.

One way to study English sentences is to recognize certain sentences as basic and other related sentences as a basic sentence plus certain statable alterations of it. Every basic English sentence has a related negative. If the basic sentence includes a modal (*can, shall, will, may, must*), a form of *have*, or a form of *be* before the verb, then the related negative is formed by adding the word *not* after the modal, *have*, or *be*:

They may come. ⟶ They may *not* come.
They have come. ⟶ They have *not* come.
They are coming. ⟶ They are *not* coming.

If the basic sentence does not include a *modal*, a form of *have*, or a form of *be* before the verb, then the related negative is formed by the addition of *not* plus a form of *do* (*do, does, did*):

She dances. ⟶ She *does not* dance.
She danced. ⟶ She *did not* dance.
They dance. ⟶ They *do not* dance.

In this section you will study *tense* in English—what it is and how it is expressed in sentences. By the end of this section you will be able to:

a) recognize verbal elements as combinations of either Present + verbal element or Past + verbal element;

b) add *present* or *past* tense to a string containing tense + be, tense + have, tense + modal, or tense + verb;

c) differentiate between indications of *tense* and indications of *time*;

d) state where and how tense is expressed in a string including tense + have, tense + modal, or tense + verb.

SECTION 2

---

32. a) The boys *smoked* cigarettes.

b) They *left* on June 26.

c) You *sang* well.

d) They *needed* money.

The italicized word in each sentence above is a combination of a particular **tense** (T) plus a particular verb. In sentences **a** to **d**, the tense that has been added to each verb is Past. In other words:

a) smoked

b) left

c) sang

d) needed

a) Past + smoke $\longrightarrow$ ....

b) Past + leave $\longrightarrow$ ....

c) Past + sing $\longrightarrow$ ....

d) Past + need $\longrightarrow$ ....

33. a) The boys *smoke* cigarettes.

b) They *leave* on June 26.

c) You *sing* well.

d) They *need* money.

In these sentences, too, the italicized word is a tense (T) plus verb combination. But in each sentence, the tense that has been added to the verb is not Past but Present (which we shall simply write as **Pres**).

a) Pres

b) Pres

c) Pres

d) Pres

a) .... + smoke $\longrightarrow$ smoke

b) .... + leave $\longrightarrow$ leave

c) .... + sing $\longrightarrow$ sing

d) .... + need $\longrightarrow$ need

tense

34. We use T as an abbreviation for ....

120

35. T is either Pres or Past. Complete the formula for each italicized word below with either Past or Pres.

a) Past

a) Down the street *rumbled* an old milk truck.
   .... + verb.

b) Pres

b. You *have* a beautiful backhand swing.
   .... + verb

c) Pres

c) She *expresses* herself effectively in writing.
   .... + verb

d) Past

d) At 8:00 sharp he *dashed* into the room.
   .... + verb

e) Past

e) He *panted* heavily.
   .... + verb

f) Pres

f) I *become* seasick on every ocean voyage.
   .... + verb

g) Past

g) He *set* a new record for the mile.
   .... + verb

Past   Pres

36. Tense can be either .... or ....

tense

37. Sentences **a** to **g** of Frame 35 all include ....
    + verb.

38. Underline the form of *be* contained in each sentence below:

a) are
b) is
c) am
d) are
e) were
f) was
g) was
h) were

a) They are leaving on June 26.
b) He is making plans.
c) I am helping her with that project.
d) They are smoking cigarettes.
e) They were leaving on June 26.
f) He was making plans.
g) I was helping her with that project.
h) They were smoking cigarettes.

39. Sentences **a** to **h** above all include

T (tense)   be

Subject + ... + ... + verb + ...

40. T + be + verb can be either

Pres

.... + be + verb

or

Past

.... + be + verb

121

was   were

am   is   are

41. Past + be ⟶ .... or ....

     Pres + be ⟶ ...., ..., or ....

42. Compare the grammatical sentence:

    a) They sing folksongs.

      Subject + T + verb + ...

with the ungrammatical sentence:

    b) They are sing folksongs.

      Subject + T + be + verb ...

The difference between **a** and **b** is the presence of *be*. But notice that the insertion of *be* necessitates a change in the verb. In order to make sentence **b** grammatical,

-ing

what must be added to the verb? - ....

43. Because *be* and *-ing* regularly co-occur in sentences like **a** to **h** (Frame 38), we will refer to them as the unit *be-ing*. That is,

    T + be + verb

can be written as

be-ing

    T + ...-............ + verb

44. If we choose the tense *Pres* and the verb *go*, the string:

    a) John + Pres + be-ing + verb

will be realized as the sentence:

    b) John is going.

The order of elements is not the same in string **a** and sentence **b**. The -ing has been moved.

    T + be-ing + verb

of the string **a** becomes:

T + be + verb + -ing

    .... + ... + ... + ...

of the sentence **b**.

45.   a) He has brought it.

      b) They have seen that movie.

      c) You have read that text.

      d) I had wondered why.

      e) They had smoked the cigarettes.

Sentences **a** to **e** all include

T   have

Subject + ... + ... + verb

46. Compare the grammatical sentence:

   a) They study French.
      Subject + T + verb + ...

with the ungrammatical sentence:

   b) They have study French.
      Subject + T + have + verb + ...

The insertion of *have* in sentences like **b** necessitates a change in the verb. You will remember that in Part Two we represented any change in a verb preceded by *have* as -en (*has gone, have brought, had put*). In order to make sentence **b** above—the sentence containing *have*—into a grammatical sentence, the -en (the change) added to the verb is the addition of / ___ /.

/əd/

47. Like *be-ing*, *have-en* can be written as a unit. Writing *have-en* in this way indicates the co-occurrence of the two elements *have* and *-en* in sentences like **a** to **e** (Frame 45): If .... precedes the verb, ... will follow it.

have   -en

48.   a) He has brought it.
    b) They have seen that movie.
    c) You have read that text.
    d) I had wondered why.
    e) They had smoked the cigarettes.

In the columns below, list the T + have-en + verb of sentences **a** to **e** above according to whether Pres or Past has been added.

Pres

| has brought |
| have seen |
| have read |

Past

| had wondered |
| had smoked |

Pres added	Past added

123

49. In sequences including T + have-en + verb, Pres or
Past is added to .... (*have* or *verb*), not
.... (*have* or *verb*).

have
verb

50. The addition of Pres to *have* is expressed as either
.... or .... Past + have
always becomes ....

has   have
had

51.

They $\left\{ \begin{array}{l} \text{a) are singing} \\ \text{b) have sung} \end{array} \right\}$ folksongs.

In sentence **a** the bracketed elements can be represented as the string:

T + be-ing + sing

which are reordered in the sentence as:

be   sing-ing

T + ... + ...-............... .

In sentence **b** the bracketed elements can be represented as the string:

T + have-en + sing

which are reordered in the sentence as:

have   sing-en

T + ... + ...-............... .

52. You may be accustomed to thinking of TENSE as
synonymous with clock or calendar **time**. Here are
some sentences including Present Tense. Notice
particularly the italicized words in each one, and
consider at what TIME the action of each sentence
occurs.

a) He *is arriving* next week.
b) The cleaning lady *comes* every Thursday.
c) They *have* always *paid* on time before.
d) He *owns* the big house on the corner.

In sentence **a**, is the *arriving* taking place at this present
moment? Clearly not, yet it contains Pres. The sentence specifically states that the arrival will occur at
a future time—*next week*. In sentence **b**, the cleaning
lady is not *coming* at the moment when the sentence is
spoken. We understand that her *coming* has regularly

occurred for some unspecified period of time in the past, and that her *coming* will continue to occur at regular intervals for some unstated period of time in the future. Certainly the speaker of sentence **b** does not intend us to think that the cleaning lady is on her way to his home at the moment of his speaking. However, sentence **b** clearly contains Pres.

The word *before* in sentence **c** tells us quite clearly that the *paying* in that sentence has taken place for some period of time in the past. There is no mention of what is happening at the moment of speaking (although the implication is that a habit of punctuality has been broken). Yet the *have* contains Pres, not Past. And it is clear that the final sentence, sentence **d**, is not intended simply to convey the meaning that the *owning* of the house is taking place at this present moment. The *owning* began at some time in the past and continues through the moment of speaking and, presumably, will continue for some time into the future.

tense   (The action of *working* may or may not take place at a future time, namely, tomorrow.)

In the sentence, *They were working yesterday*, both the TENSE (Past + be) and the TIME of *were working* are past. But in the sentence, *I wish I* **were working** *with you tomorrow*, only the .... (*time* or *tense*) of *were working* is past.

53. We can include an infinite number of clock or calendar TIMES in English sentences (e.g., *a long time ago*, *last month*, *next week*, *10 after 8*, *tomorrow morning*, *in the past*). But there are only two English TENSES:

Past   Pres

.... and ....

54. Pres and Past are *not* considered here as signals of past or present *time*. Pres and Past are simply grammatical forms that are elements of the verb phrase— and every English sentence contains either Past or Pres. Pres and Past could just as easily have been called X forms and Y forms, or type I forms and type II forms. However, following traditional terminology, we use the labels Past and Pres. It is true that the *tenses* Pres and Past frequently do coincide with present and past *times* of actions. The sports

announcer uses Pres forms in relating actions occurring at the present moment in time.

Jones takes it in. He dribbles down the court. He passes to Dugan. Dugan Shoots. It's in! The crowd goes wild!

But sentences **a** to **d** of Frame 52 show that it is not accurate to equate Pres and Past tense with present and past time because ....

....

....

in many cases, Pres and Past do not coincide with present or past time

55. T is a part of every verb phrase. Complete these formulas we have studied:

1) T
2) T
3) T
4) T

1) .... + M + verb
2) .... + have-en + verb
3) .... + be-ing + verb
4) .... + verb

56. Choose from the following list the formula that represents the italicized part of sentences **a** to **f** below.

Pres + verb   Past + verb
Pres + be-ing + verb   Past + be-ing + verb
Pres + have-en + verb   Past + have-en + verb

a) He *had missed* his bus.
....

a) Past + have-en + verb

b) I'*m practicing* that song now.
....

b) Pres + be-ing + verb

c) Bob *spends* his money foolishly.
....

c) Pres + verb

d) They *were dancing*.
....

d) Past + be-ing + verb

e) Last winter we *sold* that house.
....

e) Past + verb

f) You *have seen* that play before.
....

f) Pres + have-en + verb

57. The five modals we have had so far are all instances of Pres + modal; that is,

Pres + may ⟶ ....may..........

can   Pres + can ⟶ ....

will   Pres + will ⟶ ....

shall   Pres + shall ⟶ ....

must   Pres + must ⟶ ....

58. We say that *will* and *shall*, as in the sentences:

> *They will leave tomorrow.*

and

> *We shall miss them.*

are examples of *Pres + will* and *Pres + shall*. Thus, both contain present TENSE but refer to *future*

time   ....

59. Past added to the modals (excluding *must*) gives *might, could, would, should*.

Pres + may ⟶ may

Pres + can ⟶ can

Pres + will ⟶ will

Pres + shall ⟶ shall

might   Past + may ⟶ ....

could   Past + can ⟶ ....

would   Past + will ⟶ ....

should Past + shall ⟶ ....

60. We say that *would* and *should*, as in the sentences:

> *They would miss them.*

and

> *We should leave tomorrow.*

are examples of *Past + will* and *Past + shall*. Thus, both contain Past TENSE but refer to some

future   .... TIME.

127

61. Following the example given, write the correct formula for the italicized words of each sentence below:

EXAMPLE: He *may sell* it.   Pres + may + verb

a) Past + may + verb
b) Pres + will + verb
c) Pres + can + verb
d) Past + shall + verb
e) Pres + shall + verb
f) Past + will + verb
g) Past + can + verb

a) He *might sell* it. ....
b) He *will sell* it. ....
c) He *can sell* it. ....
d) He *should sell* it. ....
e) He *shall sell* it. ....
f) He *would sell* it. ....
g) He *could sell* it. ....

62.

He {
a) swallows
b) is swallowing
c) has swallowed
d) may swallow
e) can swallow
f) will swallow
g) shall swallow
} his medicine.

a) swallows   e) can
b) is   f) will
c) has   g) shall
d) may

Tense in all the above sentences is Pres. Suppose you wanted to change these sentences so that T was Past instead of Pres. In each sentence, underline the word that you would have to change in order to alter the tense from Pres to Past.

63. You may be used to regarding sentences as strings of words. If so, you would think of the sentence:

People eat fish.

as being composed of the three words: *people* (a noun), *eat* (a verb), and *fish* (a noun). But for our purpose of grammatical study, we see that sentences are more helpfully viewed as strings of grammatical elements that may or may not coincide with words. In the above sentence, the word *people* coincides with the grammatical element noun. But the word *eat* does not coincide with one grammatical element; rather, it is a combination of the two grammatical elements, *tense* and *verb*. Thus we regard the sentence:

People eat fish.

as a string of elements:

tense   verb

noun + ... + ... + noun

128

64.

The above sentences can be regarded grammatically as composed of the elements:

noun + ...

T

a) verb
b) M + verb
c) have-en + verb
d) be-ing + verb

$$+ \begin{cases} \text{a)} & .... \\ \text{b)} \quad .... + & .... \\ \text{c)} \quad .... + & .... \\ \text{d)} \quad .... + & .... \end{cases} + \text{noun}$$

a) 4 (pronoun + T + verb + noun)

b) 5 (pronoun + T + be-ing + verb + noun)

c) 4 (noun + T + M + verb)

d) 4 (noun + T + have-en + verb)

65. Beside each sentence below, write the number of grammatical elements (not words) it includes.

a) They like tennis. ....
b) He is drinking milk. ....
c) Jerry should study. ....
d) Janet has arrived. ....

66. Looking again at the sentences of Frame 62, tell whether the following statement is true or false:

"T can be expressed in the form of a verb, a modal, have, or be."

.... (true or false)

true

67. The part of sentence **a** (Frame 62) that you underlined can be represented as T + verb. How would you represent the portions you underlined in sentences **b** to **g**?

T + be

T + have

T + M

Sentence **b** .... + ... + verb
Sentence **c** .... + ... + verb
Sentences **d** to **g** .... + ... + verb

M   have

be   verb

68. T can be expressed in a ...., in ...., in ...., or in a ....; T will always be expressed in whichever of these four elements immediately follows it in a basic sentence.

69. In the sentence:

Peter has found his shoe.

have

T

T is expressed in .... because that is the element that immediately follows ....

SUMMARY OF FRAMES 32–69

Tense is included in the verb phrase of every English basic sentence. Present (Pres) and Past are the two realizations of tense, the two grammatical forms that sometimes *do* and sometimes *do not* coincide with present or past times of actions.

The tense in a sentence including $T + be\text{-}ing + verb$ will be added to *be*: If the tense is *Pres*, $T + be$ will be realized as *is*, *am*, or *are*; if the tense is *Past*, $T + be$ will be realized as *was* or *were*. In sentences including $T + have\text{-}en + verb$, tense is added to *have*, resulting in the form *have* or *has* if the tense is Pres, and in the form *had* if the tense is Past. And in sentences containing $T + modal + verb$, the tense will be added to modal, resulting either in a *Pres + modal* form (*can, will, shall, may, must*) or a *Past + modal* form (*could, would, should, might*). Thus the tense of a verb phrase is always indicated by the form of the verbal element that immediately follows it, regardless of whether that element is a *be* (T + be-ing...), a *have* (T + have-en...), a modal (T + M...), or a verb (T + verb...).

130

In this section you will study the composition of the verb phrase. By the end of this section you will be able to:

SECTION 3

a) identify the parts of the verb phrase in sentences;
b) interpret and produce diagrams representing the verb phrase of sentences;
c) arrange verb phrase elements in their proper order;
d) state (in the proper order) the required and optional elements that comprise verb phrases.

---

70. In the sentence:

    We'll leave after lunch.

it is the modal that
immediately follows T

T is expressed in the modal because ....

....

71. If we consider all basic sentences as having two major segments, we can represent them as follows:

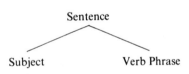

In the previous pages you have been studying the **Verb Phrase** (VP) part of sentences. You have learned that all VP's contain at least T and a Verb. Many VP's include more than these two elements. It is convenient to divide the VP into two parts, one that includes T and another that includes the Verb:

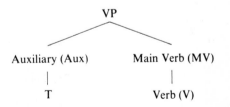

The part of the VP that always contains T is called the

Auxiliary   Aux

.... (or ....), and the part of the VP that always includes the Verb is called the

Main Verb   MV

.... (or ....).

131

72. Letting dots (…) represent additional elements optionally present after the verb, complete this diagram:

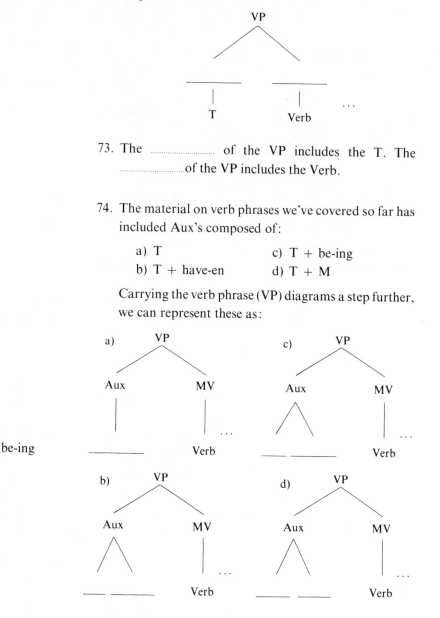

Aux   MV

Aux
MV

73. The .... of the VP includes the T. The .... of the VP includes the Verb.

74. The material on verb phrases we've covered so far has included Aux's composed of:

     a) T   c) T + be-ing
     b) T + have-en   d) T + M

Carrying the verb phrase (VP) diagrams a step further, we can represent these as:

a) T   c) T   be-ing

b) T   have-en
d) T   M

75. Beside each sentence below, write the letter of the diagram (**a** to **d** in the preceding frame) that would represent the Aux of the sentence.

a) d
b) c
c) a

     a) Next week I'll remember. ....
     b) We were swimming in the lake. ....
     c) She traveled through Europe last summer. ....

132

d) a

e) c

f) b

g) d

d) They came for dinner. ....

e) The cat was warming himself by the fire. ....

f) We've brought the slides with us. ....

g) You should study harder. ....

76. Every verb phrase can be said to consist of

Aux   MV

.... + ...

77. Aux can consist of

T

T + be-ing

T + have-en

T + M

....

.... + ...

.... + ...

.... + ...

(These are not the only possibilities.)

T

78. The first element of every Aux is ....

79. What other combinations of Aux elements occur in English? The only combinations we have dealt with so far are T plus one other Aux element (T + M, T + have-en, or T + be-ing); but many other combinations are possible. The two sentences below include new combinations of Aux elements. Complete the verb phrase diagram and the verb phrase formula for each sentence.

a) They *must have left* yesterday.

a)

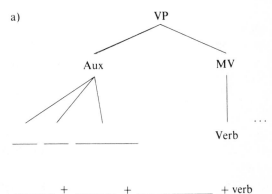

a) T   M   have-en

T + M + have-en

____ ____ _____   _____ | Verb

____ + ____ + _____ + verb

133

b) Surely he *will be coming* soon.

b)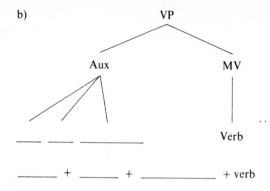

b) T   M   be-ing

T + M + be-ing

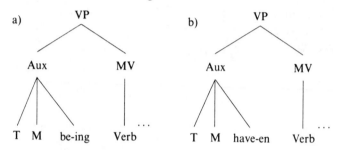

80. Study these two diagrams:

a) ⋀VP   b) ⋀VP
   Aux   MV   Aux   MV
   T M be-ing Verb ...   T M have-en Verb ...

Given that T = *Past*, M = *May*, and the verb is *find*, complete the two sentences:

a) might be finding

a) He ....
the assignments too difficult.

b) might have found

b) He ....
the assignments too difficult.

81. When T is the only Aux element in a basic sentence,

verb or MV

it is expressed in the ....

82. But if Aux includes T + M and/or have-en and/or be-ing, then T will be expressed in whichever Aux

follows

element immediately .... it.

83. What about the -en (of have-en) and the -ing (of be-ing)? Where are they expressed in verb phrases?

EXAMPLE:

He + T + M + be + -ing + find + the assignment too difficult

becomes

He might be finding the assignment too difficult.

134

He + T + M + have+-en + find + the assignment too difficult

becomes

He might have found the assignment too difficult.

In these two sentences, the -ing and -en immediately follow, and are expressed in, the ....

verb

84. T is added to whatever element follows it. The -en of have-en is also attached to whatever element follows it, and, finally, the -ing of be-ing is added to the verb that follows it. If all elements of the Aux were present in a sentence, these attachments could be diagrammed as follows:

$$\text{T} + \text{M} + \text{have}(\text{-en}) + \text{be}(\text{-ing}) + \text{verb}$$

Which element would T be attached to in these strings?

a) be
b) have
c) M
d) have

a) T + be-ing + V
b) T + have-en + V
c) T + M + V
d) T + have-en + be-ing + V

85. Which element would -en be attached to in these strings?

a) V
b) be
c) be

a) T + have-en + V
b) T + have-en + be-ing
c) T + M + have-en + be-ing + V

86. They have been here before.

be

    -en is expressed in ....

They may arrive late.

M

    T is expressed in ....

She'll be marrying Philip.

V

    -ing is expressed in ....

They had gone already.

V
have

    -en is expressed in ....
    T is expressed in ....

135

87. The sentence *He might have been finding* . . . (see Frame 80) includes the complete Aux. We can diagram the complete Aux as:

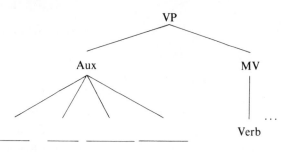

T   M
have-en   be-ing

88. Several elements of our diagram can be further specified for the sentence, *He might have been finding the assignments too difficult.* If we specify which T, which M, and which verb we have chosen, we have the diagram:

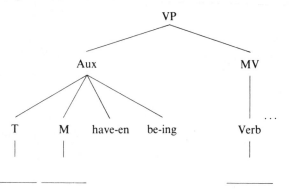

Past   may   find

89. Complete the following sentences as indicated by the corresponding diagrams.

a)

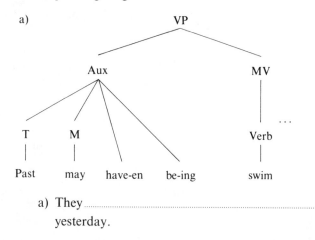

a) might have been
   swimming

a) They ....
   yesterday.

136

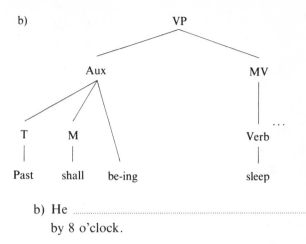

b)

b) should be sleeping

b) He ....
by 8 o'clock.

90. Complete the diagram for the italicized words:

They *could have been studying*.

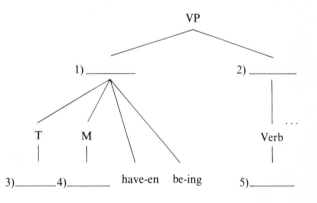

1) Aux   2) MV

3) Past   4) can
5) study

91. T + M + have-en + be-ing + verb is the representation of one possible string of VP elements. This string of grammatical elements is certainly not pronounceable! But we know that the VP we pronounce as the four words *might have been swimming* is composed of the string of elements:

    Past + may + have-en + be-ing + verb

Pres   be-ing

Past   shall

have-en

We know that the VP written as *are going* is composed of the elements .... + ... + verb, and *should have arrived* is composed of the elements .... + ... + ... + verb.

137

92. Complete the diagrams for the italicized parts of the sentences below.

   a) He *might have been going* there daily.

a)

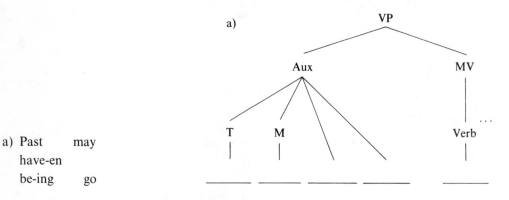

a) Past   may
   have-en
   be-ing   go

   b) You *should have seen* him.

b)

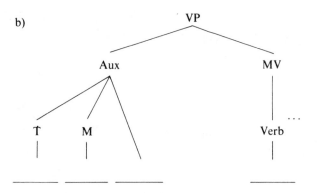

b) Past   shall
   have-en   see

   c) They *may be studying* now

c)

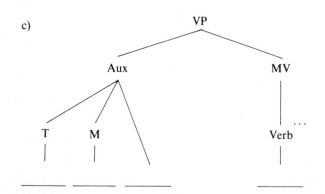

c) Pres   may
   be-ing   study

138

d) She *had been taking* swimming lessons.

d)

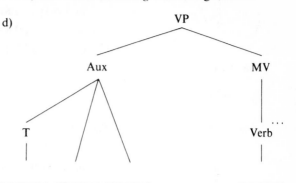

d) Past   have-en
   be-ing   take

e) Next year, I *will have been playing* the piano for ten years.

e)

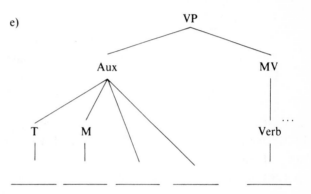

e) Pres + will + have-en
   + be-ing + play

f) We'*re planning* a trip for the fall.

f)

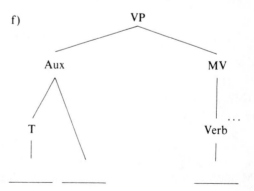

f) Pres + be-ing + plan

93. Here is an abbreviated statement of what a VP (Aux + MV) can include:

T + M + have-en + be-ing + verb

(M)   (have-en)
(be-ing)

Enclose each of the three optional elements in parentheses (   ).

139

T   V

M   have-en
be-ing

94. A VP, then, always includes two required elements and may include any or all of three optional elements. That is, a VP always includes .... and ....; and in addition, it may include any or all of the elements .... , ... , and ....

95. The order of Aux elements is always the same, regardless of how many or which of the elements are included in a given verb phrase. The order of Aux elements must be:

T   (M)
(have-en)   (be-ing)

.... + (...............) +
(...............) + (...............)

T   M

96. If Aux included only the elements M and T, the order of those elements would be .... + ... Arrange the following:

Aux includes:	*Ordered as:*

a) T, M, be-ing
b) T, have-en
c) T, M, have-en
d) T, M, be-ing
e) T, M, have-en,
   be-ing

a) be-ing, T, M   .... + ... + ...
b) T, have-en   .... + ...
c) M, have-en, T   .... + ... + ...
d) M, T, be-ing   .... + ... + ...
e) have-en M, ... + ... + ...
   be-ing, T   + ...

97. Write the formula for Aux, indicating in the proper order all the elements that can possibly occur, and which ones are optional.

T + (M) + (have-en)
+ (be-ing)

.... + ... + ...
+ ....

that M, have-en and
be-ing are optional

98. The parentheses in the Aux formula of the preceding frame indicate ....
....

140

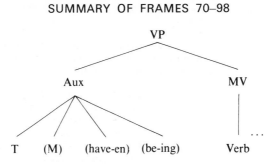

This simple diagram summarizes the information of the last section.

1) The two main parts of the verb phrase are the auxiliary and the main verb.

2) The main verb includes at least a verb.

3) The auxiliary always contains tense and can optionally include any or all of the elements modal, have-en, and be-ing.

4) The order of occurring auxiliary elements is: tense, modal, have-en, be-ing.

The -en (of have-en) and the -ing (of be-ing) attach to the verb or the Aux elements that immediately follow.

In this section you will learn some generalizations about the formation of negatives and questions. By the end of this section you will be able to:

a) state the conditions for the addition of *do*: in the formation of negatives, and yes/no and tag questions from basic sentences;

b) list the five elements that can indicate tense, and tell under what conditions each is the "tense-carrier";

c) form negatives, and yes/no and tag questions from basic sentences by applying regular steps involving the addition and rearrangement of sentence elements.

---

99. In our earlier discussion of grammatically related sentences, we used the basic sentence:

The boy smoked a cigarette behind the barn yesterday.

T   The Aux of this sentence consists simply of ....

100. Had we chosen additional Aux elements, we could have had a different basic sentence. If we had chosen T + M + have-en (with T = Past and M + can), then our basic sentence would have been: *The boy*

could have smoked   ....

a cigarette behind the barn yesterday.

101. If we had chosen T + have-en + be-ing as the Aux (with T = Past), our basic sentence would have been:

had been smoking   *The boy* ....

a cigarette behind the barn yesterday.

102. If we had chosen T + M + have-en + be-ing as the Aux (where T = Pres and M = may), our basic sentence would have been: *The boy* ....

may have been smoking   .... *a cigarette behind the barn yesterday.*

103. We learned earlier that basic sentences including:

M   T + ...

have   T + ...

be   T + ...

are made negative simply by adding *not*.

104. The following sentences have been made negative by the simple addition of *not*. For each one, tell what Aux elements precede *not*.

   EXAMPLE: The army may not have been retreating.
   T + M

a) T + have

b) T + M

c) T + have

a) The army has not been retreating. ....

b) The army should not be retreating. ....

c) The army had not been retreating. ....

105. Notice that Aux in the sentences of the last frame includes more than T and one additional element. But no matter how many elements Aux contains, *not* follows the first element after ....

T

106. If we let X stand for everything that follows T + M or T + have or T + be, what would X represent in the following formulas?

a) -en + verb

b) -ing + verb

c) have-en + verb

d) be-ing + verb

e) verb

a) T + have-en + verb ....

b) T + be-ing + verb ....

c) T + M + have-en + verb ....

d) T + M + be-ing + verb ....

e) T + M + verb ....

107. We are now ready to make a general rule about the negation of the basic sentences of English that contain more than just T in the Aux.

$$T + \begin{Bmatrix} M \\ have \\ be \end{Bmatrix} + X \qquad becomes$$

not

$$T + \begin{Bmatrix} M \\ have \\ be \end{Bmatrix} + \text{........................} + X$$

108. But let's see what happens when we negate a sentence in which T is the only Aux element.

   The army + T + retreat ⟶
   The army + T + not + retreat.

   How is tense to be expressed in this negative sentence? We know that T is expressed in the verb or the Aux element immediately following T. In the negative sentence above, is T immediately followed by a verb or an Aux element? .... (*yes* or *no*)

no

109. T cannot be added to the element immediately following it in the above string because that element (*not*) is neither a(n) .... nor a(n) .... element.

verb   Aux

110. In sentence strings in which T is not followed by a verb or an Aux element (M, have, be), we must add *do*. *Not* has been added to the following strings. To which of these strings must we also add *do*?

    a) The tiger + T + have-en + not + scare + the hunter.

    b) The tiger + T + be-ing + not + scare + the hunter.

    c) The tiger + T + not + scare + the hunter.

    d) The tiger + T + M + not + have-en + be-ing + scare + the hunter.

    e) The tiger + T + have-en + not + be-ing + scare + the hunter.

    f) The tiger + T + M + not + have-en + scare + the hunter.

c

111. We added *do* to sentence **c** above because, in that string, T was not followed by ....

a verb or an Aux element
(M, have, or be)

112. T + do can be further specified as Pres + do or Past + do.

do

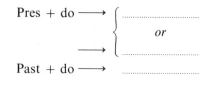

Pres + do ⟶ ....
                  or
         ⟶ ....

does
did

Past + do ⟶ ....

113. In a sentence string requiring *do*, the word is inserted immediately after ....

T

114. Underline the word that indicates the tense of each sentence below.

a) missed

b) might

c) had

d) was

e) did

a) Alex missed too many classes.

b) Alex might miss too many classes.

c) Alex has missed too many classes.

d) Alex was missing too many classes.

e) Alex did not miss too many classes.

115. The tense of a sentence can be indicated by the form of:

a) verb   d) be

b) M   e) do

c) have

a) ....   d) ....

b) ....   e) ....

c) ....

116. *Do* (*do*, *does*, or *did*) is sometimes called a tense-carrier. Why do you think *do* is given this label? What is its only function in a negative sentence?

T is expressed in the form of *do*. It indicates the Tense (Past or Pres) of the sentence in the absence of M, have, or be.

....

....

....

....

117. Let's start with some basic sentences and take them through the necessary steps to make them negative.

EXAMPLE: *The cat climbed the tree.*
    can be represented by the string:

a) *The cat + Past + climb + the tree.*
    which becomes (by adding *not*):

b) *The cat + Past + not + climb + the tree.*
    which becomes (by adding *do*):

c) *The cat + Past + do + not + climb + the tree.*
    which results in the sentence:

d) *The cat did not climb the tree.*

Take the following sentences through the same steps shown in the example. (NOTE: If step **c** is not required, skip it and go directly to **d**.)

1) *Henry could attend the meeting.*
    can be represented by the string:

a) Past + can + attend

a) Henry + ... + can + ... + the meeting. $\longrightarrow$

145

b) Past + can + not +
attend
c) (not necessary)
d) Henry could not attend
the meeting.

b) Henry + ... + ... + ...
+ .... + the meeting ⟶
c) .... ⟶
d) ....
....

2) *Those men should have been digging there.* ⟶

a) Past + shall + have-en
+ be-ing + dig
b) Past + shall + not +
have-en + be-ing +
dig
c) (not necessary)
d) Those men should not
have been digging there

a) Those men + ...
.... + there ⟶
b) Those men + ...
.... + there ⟶

c) .... ⟶
d) ....
....

3) *I know why.* ⟶

a) Pres + know
b) Pres + not + know
c) I + Pres + do + not
+ know + why
d) I do not know why.

a) I + ... + why ⟶
b) I + ... + why ⟶
c) .... ⟶
....
d) ....

4) *She's been working too hard.* ⟶

a) Pres + have-en +
be-ing + work
b) Pres + have-en +
not + be-ing + work
c) (not necessary)
d) She has not been
working too hard.

a) She + ... +
too hard ⟶
b) She + ... +
too hard ⟶
c) .... ⟶
d) ....
....

118. Consider these sentences:

    a) The tiger *could* have scared the hunter.
    b) The tiger *has* been scaring the hunter.
    c) The tiger *is* scaring the hunter.

The formulas that represent the italicized portion of sentences **a** to **c** are:

a) Past + M

b) Pres + have

c) Pres + be

a) ....
b) ....
c) ....

119. Related to the sentences **a** to **c** of the last frame are questions we ask that require a *yes* or *no* answer. They are:

    a) *Could* the tiger have scared the hunter?
    b) *Has* the tiger been scaring the hunter?
    c) *Is* the tiger scaring the hunter?

We could represent these three **yes/no** questions as:

a) Past + M

b) Pres + have

c) Pres + be

120. A simple rearrangement rule will account for the basic sentences of Frame 118 becoming the yes/no questions of Frame 119.

T + M

T + have

T + be

T + M

T + have

T + be

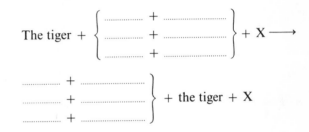

121. To form a yes/no question from a sentence containing T + M, T + have, or T + be, we simply move the T + M, T + have, or T + be to ....

....

the front of the sentence

122. In the sentence, *The tiger scared the hunter*, the only element in the Aux is T. We can represent this sentence as the string:

    The tiger + T + X

Moving T to the beginning of this string we get:

T + the tiger

    .... + ... + X

123. In the discussion of negation, we discovered that if T is not followed by a verb or an Aux element we must add .... In the string, *T + the tiger + X*,

do

no

is T followed by a verb or an Aux element? ....
(*yes* or *no*)

147

124. The string T + *the tiger* + X ⟶

T + do

.... + ... + the tiger + X

125. We can now see the formation of yes/no questions in terms of a number of simple steps.

EXAMPLE: *The cat caught the rat.*

can be represented by the string:

a) *The cat + Past + catch the rat.*
which becomes (by rearrangement):
b) *Past + the cat + catch the rat.*
which becomes (by adding *do*):
c) *Past + do + the cat + catch the rat.*
which results in the sentence:
d) *Did the cat catch the rat?*

Do these. (NOTE: Skip step **c**, the addition of *do*, if it is not applicable.)

1) *The child was holding a doll.* ⟶

a) Past + be

a) The child + ... + ... + holding a doll ⟶

b) Past + be + the child

b) .... + ... + ... + holding a doll ⟶

c) (not necessary)

c) .... ⟶

d) Was the child holding a doll?

d) ....

2) *I should have taken notes.* ⟶

a) Past + shall

a) I + ... + ... + have taken notes ⟶

b) Past + shall + I

b) .... + ... + ... + have taken notes ⟶

c) (not necessary)

c) .... ⟶

d) Should I have taken notes?

d) ....

3) *Joe found the money on the floor.* ⟶

a) Past

a) Joe + ... + find the money on the floor ⟶

b) Past + Joe

b) .... + ... + find the money on the floor ⟶

c) Past + do + Joe +
   find the money on the
   floor
d) Did Joe find the money
   on the floor?

a) Pres + have

b) Pres + have + they

c) (not necessary)
d) Have they seen that
   movie?

c) .... ⟶
   ....

d) ....
   ....

4) *They have seen that movie.* ⟶

a) They + ... + ... + seen
   that movie ⟶
b) .... + ... + ...
   + seen that movie ⟶
c) .... ⟶
d) ....
   ....

126. We have another type of question in English that is
     related to basic sentences. Compare these pairs of
     sentences:

     a) He should have kept the appointment.
     b) He should have kept the appointment, shouldn't
        he?
     c) Jan has been taking Russian.
     d) Jan has been taking Russian, hasn't he?
     e) You are leaving town tonight.
     f) You are leaving town tonight, aren't you?

     The second sentence of each pair is called a **tag
     question**. Provide the related tag question for each
     basic sentence below:

The students can memorize
the lines by tomorrow,
can't they?

The boy has delivered the
newspaper, hasn't he?

Jim is dating Marie,
isn't he?

The students can memorize the lines by tomorrow.
....
....

The boy has delivered the newspaper.
....
....

Jim is dating Marie.
....
....

127. What did you do to change the basic sentences into
     tag questions? One thing you did was to supply the
     appropriate **pronoun** form of the subject in the tag

149

part of the question. You also repeated the T +

M   have   be

.... or T + ... or T + ...

of the basic sentence.

-n't

128. You also added .... to all three tags.

129. What is the tag question for this sentence?

Eric married Jeannette.

Eric married Jeannette,
didn't he?

....

....

130. Again, in making a tag, you've added *n't* and the appropriate pronoun form at the end. But in the

do

absence of *M*, *have*, or *be*, you added ....

131. Since the Aux of *Eric married Jeannette* consists only

T   do

of ...., it is necessary to add .... in the tag question.

132. Now consider these tag questions.

He mustn't go, must he?
He would not go, would he?

Complete these by adding the appropriate tag.

a) should he
b) has he
c) is he

a) The boy shouldn't go, ...?
b) The boy hasn't gone, ...?
c) The boy is not going, ...?

133. The Aux elements that you repeated in the tags you wrote for sentences **a** to **c** above were

a) T + M
b) T + have
c) T + be

a) .... + ...
b) .... + ...
c) .... + ...

And—as with the previous tag questions—you in-

pronoun

cluded the .... form of the subject as part of the tag.

150

134. But there is a difference between the tags of Frame 132 and the ones you studied earlier. Compare the following to find the difference:

a) He should go, shouldn't he?

and

b) He shouldn't go, should he?

You can now make your own rule about the presence of *n't* in the tags of this particular type of question. If the basic sentence has already been negated, the tag

will not

.... (*will* or *will not*) include *n't*. If

will

the basic sentence is affirmative, the tag .... (*will* or *will not*) include *n't*.

SUMMARY OF FRAMES 99–134

A simple formula describes the negation of most basic English sentences:

$$\ldots T + \left\{ \begin{array}{l} M \\ \text{have} \\ \text{be} \end{array} \right\} + X \longrightarrow \quad \ldots T + \left\{ \begin{array}{l} M \\ \text{have} \\ \text{be} \end{array} \right\} + \text{not} + X$$

Put in prose form, this rule states that a sentence whose Aux includes tense + modal, tense + have, or tense + be is negated by inserting *not* after these elements. (Notice that what precedes and follows these elements is irrelevant to the formation of negative sentences.) If Aux includes only tense, then both *do* and *not* are inserted after tense when the sentence is negated. In English sentences, tense can be added to and expressed in the form of a modal, the form of *be*, the form of *have*, the form of a verb, or, in the case of negative sentences and questions, in the form of *do* (*do*, *does*, *did*).

A basic sentence whose Aux includes T + modal, T + have, or T + be is changed into a yes/no question by moving these Aux elements to the beginning of the sentence. A basic sentence whose Aux includes only T is changed into a yes/no question by moving tense (T) to the beginning of the string and adding *do* immediately after T.

Making tag questions always involves the addition of a pronoun that corresponds to the subject of the basic sentence (Tom can go, can't *he*?, Mary and Bill can't go, can *they*?). In tag questions made from basic sentences with an Aux including only tense, *do* is added. Otherwise, the T + modal, T + have, or T + be of Aux is repeated in the tag. If the basic sentence has not already been negated, *n't* is added in the tag.

In this section we have seen that the relations between the basic form of a sentence and its negative and interrogative forms can be shown clearly and succinctly in terms of a small number of regular changes—changes such as the addition of elements, like *do* and *not*; or the rearrangement of elements, which may be accomplished by moving a T + modal, T + have, or T + be to the beginning of the sentence.

If the rules that we have discussed applied only to the formation of one related sentence, say, the negative of some sentence, then it would hardly be worth the effort to consider that relationship in terms of these rules. But we have seen that the rules involving the elements of the Aux can be applied to the formation of an infinite number of negative sentences, as well as to the formation of yes/no and tag questions. In the next section we shall see that these same rules are relevant to the formation of yet other related sentences.

But before we go on, a word about the irregularities in the grammar of sentences. The application of the rules we have learned will in most instances produce grammatical English sentences, such as *He can go, can't he?* and *He shouldn't do that, should he?* However, the application of these rules could also derive some unacceptable sentences; for example, *He may go there, mayn't he? He shalln't go, shall he? He will go, willn't he?* Special rules must be included to account for the irregular cases here, just as special rules were needed to handle irregular nouns (e.g., *foot-feet*) and irregular verbs (e.g., *eat-ate*). Since our goal is to understand how our language works, or, better, how we use our language, it is equally, if not more, important that we understand its regular aspects as well as those that are irregular.

There are other regularities of English sentence grammar, which we shall not cover in this introductory treatment of English grammar. For example, you have probably already thought of another regular type of tag question that could be described. We have looked at the rules that would account for *He can go, can't he?* Slightly different rules would account for sentences of the type *He can go, can he not?* and *He should stop, should he not?*

The rules you have already studied are important in the derivation of other related sentences. Notice that all the following questions include the changes that were examined in the derivation of yes/no questions:

1) Where *did he find it?*
2) When *will he leave?*
3) Where *has he been playing ball?*
4) When *is he bringing the news?*
5) What *did he buy?*
6) Who(m) *did the policeman arrest?*

In this section you will study the formation of *where, when, what/who(m),* and *what/who* questions. By the end of this section you will be able to:

a) form *where, when, what/who(m)* questions by applying regular replacement and rearrangement rules to basic sentences;

b) form *what/who* (subject) questions by applying the appropriate replacement rule to basic sentences;

c) state the conditions for choosing *what* or *who* or *whom* in making questions;

d) identify the words or phrases in basic sentences that can be replaced by the question words, *where, when, what, who,* and *whom*.

SECTION 5

---

135. Our original basic sentence was:

The boy smoked a cigarette behind the barn yesterday.

Changing this basic sentence to a yes/no question, we get:

Did the boy smoke a cigarette behind the barn yesterday?

....

....

136. A basic sentence can include an **adverb of place** (e.g., *there, next to the window, at the corner, someplace*). It can also include an **adverb of time** (e.g., *then, a month ago, soon, last week, next Monday, sometime*). Our basic sentence (above) includes both an adverb of

place

.... (*behind the barn*) and an adverb of

time

.... (*yesterday*).

137. Consider the following:

The boy smoked a cigarette someplace.

a)   Did the boy smoke a cigarette someplace?

b)   Did the boy smoke a cigarette where?

c) Where did the boy smoke a cigarette?

The strings **a** to **c** represent the steps that our basic sentence goes through to derive a question that asks about *location* or *place*. Having changed the statement into a yes/no question (**a**), we substitute *where* for the

place

adverb of .... (**b**) and then move

where

.... to the beginning of question (**c**).

153

138. Taking another basic sentence through the steps for *where* questions, we can begin with:

He went someplace.

yes/no	a) Did he go someplace?
replacement	b) Did he go where?
rearrange	c) Where did he go?

Take the following basic sentences through the necessary steps to produce *where* questions.

The teacher lives someplace.

a) Does the teacher live someplace?

a) ....?

b) Does the teacher live where?

b) ....?

c) Where does the teacher live?

c) ....?

You will see Bob someplace.

a) Will you see Bob someplace?

a) ....?

b) Will you see Bob where?

b) ....?

c) Where will you see Bob?

c) ....?

Mr. Jones is working someplace.

a) Is Mr. Jones working someplace?

a) ....?

b) Is Mr. Jones working where?

b) ....?

c) Where is Mr. Jones working?

c) ....?

Sally has danced someplace.

a) Has Sally danced someplace?

a) ....?

b) Has Sally danced where?

b) ....?

c) Where has Sally danced?

c) ....?

139. You can now explain the relation that we see between sentences like:

The boy smoked a cigarette behind the barn.

and

Where did the boy smoke a cigarette?

154

In addition to going through the changes to make the
basic sentence into a yes/no question, we substitute

where
at the beginning of the
sentence

the word .... for the adverb of place and
put it ....
....

140. Now consider these sentences:

> The boy smoked a cigarette sometime.

a) Did the boy smoke a cigarette sometime?

b) Did the boy smoke a cigarette when?

c) When did the boy smoke a cigarette?

To derive *When did the boy smoke a cigarette?* from
the basic sentence, *The boy smoked a cigarette sometime*, was it necessary to:

a) first apply the rules to derive a yes/no question?

a) yes

....

b) first apply the rules to make the sentence nega-

b) no

tive? ....

c) yes

c) substitute for the adverb of time? ....

d) move the substitute word to the beginning of

d) yes

the sentence? ....

141. Derive *when* questions from these basic sentences:

He plans to leave sometime.

a) Does he plan to leave
sometime?

a) ....?

b) Does he plan to leave
when?

b) ....?

c) When does he plan to
leave?

c) ....?

He was working sometime.

a) Was he working
sometime?

a) ....?

b) Was he working when?

b) ....?

c) When was he working?

c) ....?

142. We have seen that the interrogatives beginning with
where and *when* are related to basic sentences that

place   time

contain adverbs of .... and ....

155

143. Now let's consider another type of question that can be shown to be related to our basic sentence. Underline the word in sentence **b** to which *what* of sentence **a** is related:

a) *What* did the boy smoke?

something

b) The boy smoked something behind the barn yesterday.

144. In the question:

What did the boy smoke behind the barn yesterday?

have the rules to derive the yes/no question been

yes

applied? ....

145. Then the basic sentence:

The boy smoked something behind the barn yesterday.

can be said to go through the following steps to produce the *what* question:

first, change the basic sentence to a

yes/no question
something
to the beginning of the
sentence

........................../........................   .... ;

second, substitute *what* for .... ;

third, move *what* ....
....

146. Change the following sentences into questions, following the steps listed in the last frame:

The boy found something behind the barn.

a) Did the boy find something behind the barn?

a) ....
...........................?

b) Did the boy find what behind the barn?

b) ....
...........................?

c) What did the boy find behind the barn?

c) ....
...........................?

The boy caught something behind the barn.

a) Did the boy catch something behind the barn?

a) ....
...........................?

b) Did the boy catch what behind the barn?

b) ....
...........................?

c) What did the boy catch behind the barn?

c) ....
...........................?

147. The question, *What did the boy find behind the barn?* is related to the basic sentence, *The boy found something behind the barn.* What basic sentence is related to the question, *Who(m) did the boy find behind the barn?*

The boy found someone behind the barn.

....

....

148. In the question, *Who(m) did the boy find behind the barn?* the first word can be either .... or

who

whom

....

149. *Who(m)* questions are similar to *where, when,* and *what* questions in several ways. The *(m)* simply means that both *who* and *whom* are used by speakers of English as replacements for an *object* noun. In making a *who(m)* question, we begin by changing the basic sentence into a ....,

yes/no question

just as we did when we made *where, when,* and *what* questions.

150.   a) The teacher led someone down the hall.
        b) Fido bit someone in the leg.

In making sentences **a** and **b** into *who(m)* questions, our first step will be to change them into the yes/no questions:

a) Did the teacher lead someone down the hall?

a) ....
....?

b) Did Fido bite someone in the leg?

b) ....
....?

151. In making *who(m)* questions (as with *where, when,* and *what* questions), two further steps are necessary after we have made a yes/no question. The next step is (underline your choice):

a) The addition of a new element to the sentence.
b) The replacement of an element in the sentence by a new element.
c) The deletion (taking away) of an element.

b

d) A rearrangement of an element.

157

d

152. A final change will complete the steps necessary to transform the basic sentence into a *who(m)* question. The final step requires one of the choices given in the last frame. Which one? ....

153. If we apply the second step, that is, the replacement of an element in the sentences by a new element, to the yes/no questions we derived earlier:

a) Did the teacher lead someone down the hall?
b) Did Fido bite someone in the leg?

we get:

a) Did the teacher lead who(m) down the hall?
b) Did Fido bite who(m) in the leg?

a) ....
.... ?
b) ....
.... ?

who(m)
the beginning of the question

154. Finally, we apply the last step to the results of step two, that is, we move .... to ....
....

155. Applying the three rules to form *who(m)* questions to the sentence *Mary loves someone*, we would have:

a) Does Mary love someone?
b) Does Mary love who(m)?
c) Who(m) does Mary love?

first   a) .... ?

second   b) .... ?

third   c) .... ?

156. Complete the questions you think are related to these sentences:

a) Who

b) What

a) Someone hit Mary. ⟶ .... hit Mary?
b) Something hit Mary. ⟶ .... hit Mary?

157. The change from the basic sentences above to their related *who/what* questions can be described as (underline your choice):

a) The addition of a new element.
b) The replacement of an element.
c) The deletion of an element.
d) The rearrangement of an element.

b

158

158. If we make a basic sentence:

X hit Mary.

into a question by replacing X with either *who* or

who

what

what, we will choose .... if the subject is
human, and .... if the subject is nonhuman.

159. We have been using the indefinite terms *someplace*,
sometime, *someone*, and *something* in our discussion
of English question formation. These have been used
as general cover terms for expressions of *place*, *time*,
persons, and *things*. In the sentences below, we will
use particular expressions rather than indefinite ones.
Underline the words or phrases that would be replaced
by the question words given before each sentence:

last evening	WHEN?	He flew the plane through the storm last evening.
in room 205	WHERE?	They'll hold the meeting in room 205 next Thursday.
the workmen	WHO?	The workmen found a beehive under the roof.
a hot dog	WHAT?	The soldier was eating a hot dog at the counter.
under an old stump	WHERE?	The dog buried the bone under an old stump.
Steven	WHO(M)?	Tom sent Steven to the store for milk.
the car	WHAT?	The car hit Tom.

SUMMARY OF FRAMES 135–159

Basic sentences can include adverbs of place, adverbs of time, or both. There
are three steps involved in changing a basic sentence into a *where, when,* or *what,
who(m)* question:

1) The basic sentence string is turned into a yes/no question.
2) An element is replaced by a new element:
   a) adverb of time   is replaced by   *when*
   b) adverb of place   is replaced by   *where*
   c) direct object   is replaced by   *what, who, whom*
3) The replacement word is moved to the beginning of the sentence.

159

What is the replacement word for direct objects that are nonhuman, and *who* or *whom* replaces human direct objects.

In changing a basic sentence into a who/what question—a subject question (*Who/what hit Mary?*)—only one step is required, namely, the replacement of a human subject by the word *who* or a nonhuman subject by the word *what*.

In this section you will study the formation of passive sentences. By the end of this section you will be able to:

a) identify transitive verbs in sentences;
b) define *transitive verb*;
c) form passive sentences by the application of regular rearrangement and addition rules;
d) describe the process of changing a basic sentence into a passive in terms of rearrangement and addition rules.

SECTION 6

---

160. The Verb (V) in this diagram is a **transitive verb** (Vt):

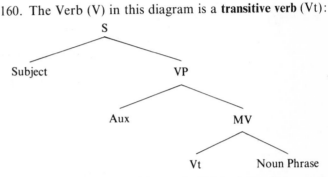

noun phrase

Sometimes a transitive verb (Vt) is defined as a verb that "takes a direct object," as in the sentence *The farmer planted **a tree***. Defining it in terms of our diagram, we can say that a Vt is a verb that, together with a ...., comprises the MV of the Verb Phrase.

161. In the sentence *The farmer planted a tree*, the **Noun Phrase** (NP) after the Vt is ....

a tree

162. Underline the NP's after the transitive verbs in these sentences:

a) the cow
b) the dog
c) the farmer
d) John
e) the lawyer

a) The farmer milked the cow.
b) The cow kicked the dog.
c) The dog bit the farmer.
d) The farmer sued John.
e) John hit the lawyer.

163. From the last frame, we can see that NP's such as *the farmer*, *the cow*, *the dog*, and *John*, that function as objects of Vt's also serve as **Subjects** of sentences. Another way of saying the same thing is: NP's function as subjects and objects in sentences. Thus a dia-

161

gram of the sentence *The farmer planted a tree* might look like this:

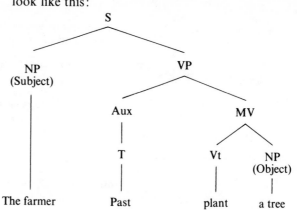

Complete this diagram to represent the sentence:

John hit the lawyer.

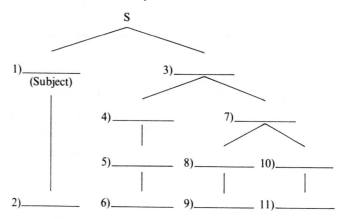

1) NP	7) MV
2) John	8) Vt
3) VP	9) hit
4) Aux	10) NP
5) T	11) the lawyer
6) Past	

164. Taking note of the several elements in the Aux, complete this diagram to represent the sentence:

The dog may have buried the bone.

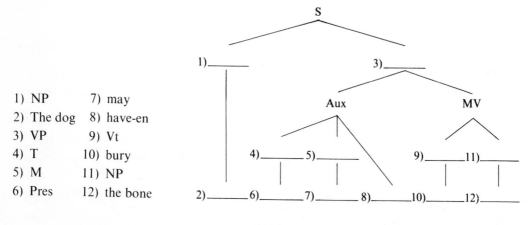

1) NP	7) may
2) The dog	8) have-en
3) VP	9) Vt
4) T	10) bury
5) M	11) NP
6) Pres	12) the bone

162

165. Which of these sentences contain a Vt?

a) The bird flew away.
b) Eleanor lost the money.
c) The hen was clucking noisily in the yard.
d) She sings hymns.
e) She sang beautifully at the recital yesterday.
f) The janitor found a five dollar bill on the floor.

b   d   f

166. A Vt is always followed by a (an) ....

NP

167. The MV of a sentence containing a transitive verb is composed of a(n) .... and a(n) ....

Vt   NP

168. Each basic sentence below in column I is an **active** sentence and has a related **passive** sentence. In column II, supply the passive forms of sentences **b** and **c**.

I	II
a) The girl found a ring.	a) A ring was found by the girl.
b) The volunteer lost a postcard.	b) ....
c) The squirrel cracked a nut.	c) ....

b) A postcard was lost
   by the volunteer.
c) A nut was cracked
   by the squirrel.

169. The basic active sentence, *The dog bit the boy*, can be represented as the string:

The dog + Past + bite + the boy

The related passive sentence can be represented by the string:

The boy + Past + be + bite + -en + by + the dog

Which of the following processes were applied to the active sentence to change it to its related passive sentence? [Underline your choice(s).]

a) addition of an element or elements
b) replacement of an element
c) deletion of an element
d) rearrangement of an element or elements

a   d

163

NP
NP

170. Notice that the elements that are rearranged when we change an active into a passive sentence are both the same type of grammatical structure—in our example, *The dog* and *The boy*. The .... that precedes the verb changes with the .... that follows the verb.

171. Putting it in a schematic way:

NP1 + Verb + NP2

becomes

2   1

NP..... + Verb + NP.....

172. Besides rearranging elements to form the passive, we noted in Frame 169 that elements were also added. Look at the elements of the active sentence:

The baseball + Past + shatter + the glass.
  (NP1)   (NP2)

then complete the passive string

be

The glass + Past + ... + shatter +
  (NP2)

-en   by

.... + ... + *the baseball.*
                                  (NP1)

173. In changing a basic sentence to its passive form, *be*
verb   is added immediately before the .... and
verb   *-en* is added immediately after the ....

174. In addition to NP1 and NP2 switching places and
by   adding *be* before and *-en* after the verb, ...
            is added before NP1 in its new position.

175. Let's carry some basic sentences through the required rules of rearrangement and addition to change them to passive sentences.

The dog chased the cat.

    a)   NP1 + Past + chase +
                                NP2 $\longrightarrow$

b) NP2   b) (rearrange)   .... + Past + chase +
   NP1   .... $\longrightarrow$

164

c) NP2
be
-en   by
NP1

c) (addition)   .... + Past +
.... + chase +
.... + ... +
....

Mrs. Appletree will sing the song.

a) NP1 + Pres + will + sing + NP2 $\longrightarrow$
b) .... + Pres + will + sing +
.... $\longrightarrow$

b) NP2
NP1
c) NP2   be
-en   by   NP1

c) .... + Pres + will + ... + sing
+ .... + ... + ... + ...

That company is selling the soap.

a) NP1 + Pres + be-ing + sell + NP2 $\longrightarrow$
b) .... + Pres + be-ing + sell +
.... $\longrightarrow$

b) NP2
NP1
c) NP2   be
-en   by   NP1

c) .... + Pres + be-ing + ... +
sell + ... + ... + ...

176. Consider passive sentences such as:

    a) The cat was chased by the dog.
    b) The song was sung by Mrs. Appletree.
    c) The soap is being sold by that company.

One further change is possible, although not required. We can delete a portion of these sentences and still have acceptable English sentences. Put parentheses around the portion of each of the above sentences that can be optionally deleted.

a) (by the dog)
b) (by Mrs. Appletree)
c) (by that company)

177. In your own words, state which portion of a sentence that has been changed to its passive form can be deleted.

The doer of the action [or]
NP1 [or] the agent [or] the
original subject.

....
....

SUMMARY OF FRAMES 160–177

A transitive verb (Vt) is one that is followed by an NP and, together with the following NP, comprises the MV of the sentence VP as in this diagram:

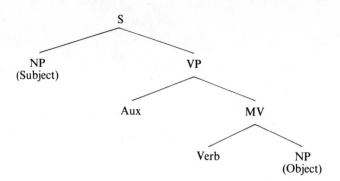

We have seen that Active sentences that contain the elements Subject + Aux + Transitive Verb + Object can be changed into Passive sentences by the application of rearrangement and addition rules: (1) switch the places of the subject NP and the object NP, and (2) add three elements, *be*, *-en*, and *by*. *Be* immediately precedes and *-en* immediately follows the Verb. *By* precedes the original subject. Of course, you knew how to form the passive of all the active sentences we have used in our examples. All that has been added is a detailed explanation of what you already knew.

In this section you will study the special properties of certain classes of verbs. By the end of this section, you will be able to:

SECTION 7

a) state the defining characteristics of transitive verbs and of nontransitive verbs, including *be*, *seem*-type, *become*-type, and intransitive verbs;

b) differentiate between transitive and nontransitive use of particular verbs.

---

178. Look at the following sentences and circle those that have related passive sentences.

    a) The boy swiped an apple.

    b) The man called a doctor.

    c) The man is a doctor.

    d) John is hungry.

    e) John is at the store.

    f) The cows are in the corn.

    g) The cows ate the corn.

a   b   g

179. Look again at the sentences of the last frame. Which contain Vt's? ....

a   b   g

180. Are sentences that contain Vt's the same as those that can be made passive (passivized)? ....

yes

181. Verbs that can be used in related active/passive sentences are transitive verbs. For now, we shall simply call those not used in related active/passive sentences **nontransitive**. Looking back at the sentences of Frame 178, we see that .... is a nontransitive verb.

be

182. The sentence *John is hungry*, which contains the nontransitive verb *be*, contains the elements:

Subject + Pres + be + Adjective (Adj)

This sentence can be diagrammed as follows:

167

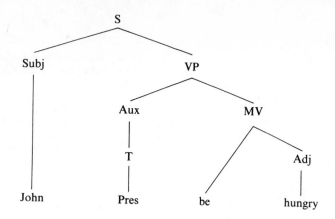

Complete this diagram to represent the sentence:

The food is terrible.

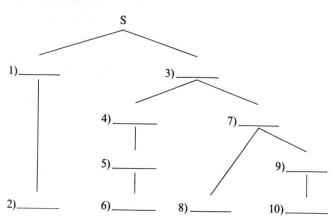

1) Subj   6) Pres
2) The food   7) MV
3) VP   8) be
4) Aux   9) Adj
5) T   10) terrible

183. In the sentences, *John is hungry* and *The food is terrible*, the verb *be* in each case is followed by a(n)

Adj

....

184. What, besides adjectives, can follow *be*? Circle the words or phrases that would be acceptable after *be* in the sentence:

The elephant is
- a) the culprit.
- b) happily.
- c) quietly.
- d) a mammal.
- e) here.
- f) in the tent.
- g) merrily.
- h) a beast.

a   d   e   f   h

168

NP
adverbs (of)
place

185. When *be* is the verb in a basic sentence, it can be followed by an Adj (*hungry, terrible*), a(n) .... (*the culprit, a mammal, a beast*), or .... of .... (*here, in the tent*).

happily   quietly
merrily

186. The three words you rejected after *be* in Frame 184 were: ...., ..., and ....

adverb (of)   manner

187. The three words you rejected after *be* are representative of another type of adverb. They are called **adverbs of manner**. When the MV of a basic sentence contains *be*, it cannot be immediately followed by an .... of ....

188. We have seen that *be* can be followed by adjectives (Adj), noun phrases (NP), and adverbs of place (Adv-pl). Identify the words or phrases that occur after *be* in the following sentences with one of the abbreviations given in the parentheses above.

a) Adj
b) NP
c) Adv-pl
d) Adv-pl
e) NP
f) Adj

a) The cat is hungry. ....
b) My son is a scout. ....
c) Our daughter isn't at home. ....
d) John and Mary are in my house. ....
e) John and Mary are thieves. ....
f) John and Mary are dangerous. ....

189. Compare these two sentences:

a) John is a scout.
b) John hit a scout.

NP

Both *be* in sentence **a** and *hit* in sentence **b** are followed by the .... *a scout*.

190. However, sentences with *be* and sentences with verbs like *hit* are different in a number of ways. One of the sentences of the last frame has a passive form. Which

b

one? .... (**a** or **b**)

191. One of the verbs, *be* or *hit*, could be followed immediately by an Adj instead of the NP *a scout*. Which

be

one? ....

Adj   NP   Adv-pl

192. We have seen that the nontransitive verb *be* can be followed by ...., ..., or ....

193. Are all nontransitive verbs like *be*? Which of the following words or phrases are acceptable after the verb *seem*?

The boy seems {

a) here.
b) a man.
c) happy.
d) under the blanket.
e) angry.
f) merrily.
g) happily.
h) a fool.

c   e   (also b and h; see next frame)

194. Unquestionably, *happy* and *angry* are acceptable after *seem*. Most speakers of English would also accept **b**, *a man*, and **h**, *a fool*. However, in American English, noun phrases (NP) after *seem* are not as common as they are in British English. We noted earlier that *be* can be followed by Adj, NP, and Adv-pl, but not by an adverb of manner (Adv-manner). Which of these four cannot follow *seem*? .... and

Adv-pl
Adv-manner

....

195. *Be* and *seem*, then, are alike in some ways and different in others. Which of these statements are true (T) and which are false (F) for *be* and *seem*?

	Be	Seem
a)	T	T
b)	T	T
c)	T	F
d)	F	F
e)	T	T

	Be	Seem
a) is nontransitive.	....	....
b) can be followed by Adj.	....	....
c) can be followed by Adv-pl.	....	....
d) can be followed by Adv-manner.	....	....
e) can be followed by NP.	....	....

196. From the last frame, we can now state that the one major difference between *be* and *seem* is that ....

be
seem

can be followed by Adv-pl but .... cannot.

170

197. Two additional nontransitive verbs that are very much like *seem* are *become* and *remain*. Circle the following words or phrases that are acceptable after *become*:

Mr. Jones became
a) angry.
b) the president.
c) on the corner.
d) uncomfortably.
e) frustrated.
f) a man.
g) notorious.

a   b   e   f   g

198. Identify each word or phrase after *become* in the last frame with one of these abbreviations: NP, Adv-pl, Adv-manner, or Adj.

a) Adj
b) NP
c) Adv-pl
d) Adv-manner
e) Adj
f) NP
g) Adj

a) ....
b) ....
c) ....
d) ....
e) ....
f) ....
g) ....

199. From the last two frames, we can see that *become* (and *remain*) can be followed by .... and ...., but not by .... and .... The essential difference between *seem* and *become* is the complete freedom of occurrence of NP after ....

Adj   NP

Adv-pl   Adv-manner

become

200. We will look at just one more type of nontransitive verb. Circle the following words or phrases that are acceptable after *arrive* in the sentence:

The letter arrived
a) yesterday
b) the man.
c) a scout.
d) on Tuesday.
e) the mailbox.
f) blue.
g) in an envelope.

a   d   g

171

201. Of the three acceptable words or phrases in the last frame, two are **adverbs of time**. They are

yesterday   on Tuesday   .... and ....

202. The other phrase is an Adv-pl. Among the rejected words and phrases in Frame 200 are the NP's

the man   a scout   ...., ..., and
the mailbox   blue   ...., and the Adj ....

203. Verbs like *arrive*, unlike any of the other verbs we have considered, cannot be followed by NP. *Arrive*, as well as hundreds of other verbs in English, represents the major class of nontransitive verbs. This class is more generally called **intransitive**. Below are six sentences, some of which contain intransitive verbs. Mark with Vt those sentences that contain transitive verbs, and with Vi those that contain intransitive verbs:

a) Vt   a) John closed the door. ....
b) Vi   b) Mary swims in the morning. ....
c) Vt   c) The rattlesnake bit the mongoose. ....
d) Vt   d) My wife spilled the coffee. ....
e) Vi   e) My dog sleeps under the bed. ....
f) Vt   f) He sharpened his pencil. ....

204. We have noted that verbs can be divided into two major groups, transitive and nontransitive. Furthermore the nontransitive can be subdivided into *be* as a separate class; then come verbs like *seem*, and finally the large class of intransitive verbs. Some verbs are found in both transitive and intransitive divisions. The verbs *taste*, *sound*, and *feel*, for example, can be used both as transitive and intransitive verbs. Indicate with either Vi (for intransitive) or Vt (for transitive) the function of the verbs in these sentences.

a) Vt   a) He tasted the apple. ....
b) Vi   b) The apples tasted good. ....
c) Vi   c) His voice sounds awful. ....
d) Vt   d) The police sounded the alarm. ....
e) Vi   e) I feel wonderful today. ....
f) Vt   f) The doctor felt his forehead. ....

We have learned that sentences in English are made up of Subjects + Verb Phrases. Furthermore, we learned that every VP is made up of an Aux and an MV, and that every MV contains a Verb. In the past few pages, it has been demonstrated that different verbs have different properties. That is, some verbs occur in sentences that can be changed into passives. We have called these transitive verbs. They are simply verbs that take direct objects like *the boy* or *an apple*, or even *the old lady who lives next door*, and, by the application of simple rules, can be changed to the subject of related passive sentences. For example, the active sentence, *He loves the old lady who lives next door*, can be changed to the passive, *The old lady who lives next door is loved by him*. We called verbs that do not have this property *nontransitive*. Again, by looking at the elements that could follow certain verbs, we saw that *be* was the only verb that could be followed immediately by adjectives, noun phrases, and adverbs of place. This puts it into a class different from *seem* and *become*, which can be followed by adjectives and nouns but not by adverbs of place. *Arrive*, like *swim*, *walk*, *fly*, *smile*, and many other verbs, can be followed by adverbs of place and other adverbs, but not immediately by adjectives and noun phrases.

There are additional verbs and verb classes that could be established in a more extensive presentation. The classification we have examined provides a beginning to an understanding of the different kinds of sentences that occur in English.

In this section you will study:

a) one way to combine simple sentences;
b) the use of *who, whom, which,* and *that* as substitute words;
c) the possibility of deleting a substitute word;
d) a review of the rules that account for the relations between basic sentences and nonbasic sentences.

SECTION 8

---

205. Very seldom do we talk or write using only the very short sentences that we have used as examples in this program. But many of the longer, more complicated sentences of English can be understood by studying these basic sentence types. Compare these three sentences.

     a) My aunt is very wealthy.
     b) My aunt lives in Chicago.
     c) My aunt who lives in Chicago is very wealthy.

yes

Does sentence **c** contain all the information of sentences **a** and **b**? ....

206. We could say that sentence **c** of the last frame is a combination of sentences **a** and **b**. If it is, then we can provide rules for combining sentences **a** and **b** to form **c**. What word occurs in **c** that does not occur in either

who

a or **b**? ....

207. Instead of repeating the NP (*my aunt*) of sentence **b**, one of the following processes is applied:

     a) addition of an element
     b) replacement of an element
     c) deletion of an element

b

     d) rearrangement of an element

208. After replacing the repeated NP with *who*, sentence **b** was inserted or embedded in sentence **a**, thus:

lives in Chicago

My aunt who ....
is very wealthy.

174

209. Combine sentences **a** and **b** below, following the steps outlined above.

    a) The doctor just arrived.
    b) The doctor performed the operation.

    1) Substitute *who* for the repeated NP.

who performed the operation

....

    2) Embed the sentence with *who* into sentence **a**.

The doctor who performed the operation just arrived.

....

....

210. Can the same rules be applied to combine these two sentences?

    a) The dog belongs to Mrs. Jones.
    b) The dog chased the mailman.

no

....

211. Sentences **a** and **b** of the last frame can be combined much as the sentences of Frames 205 and 209. However, when the repeated NP is not **human** we cannot use *who* as a replacement, but must use either

which   that

.... or ....

212. Let's look at these two sentences.

    a) The doctor charged me $100.
    b) You recommended the doctor.

The repeated NP in sentences **a** and **b** is ....

the doctor

....

213. In sentence **b**, *the doctor* is the ....

object

of the .... verb *recommend*.

transitive

214. When the repeated NP is the object of the sentence we wish to embed, we substitute *who(m)* (if it is human). Applying this rule to sentence **b** of Frame 212 would

you recommended whom

give ....

215. After the substitution of *who(m)* for the repeated NP that is the object of the sentence to be embedded, we

the beginning of the sentence

must move *who(m)* to ....

who(m) you recommended

.... , giving ....

....

The doctor who(m) you
recommended charged me
$100.

216. Now we are ready to embed sentence **b** into sentence **a**, giving us the combined sentence:

....

....

217. The sentence, *The doctor whom you recommended charged me* $100, is then a combination of two short simple sentences. There is an additional step that can be optionally taken with this sentence. Compare the following:

    a) The doctor whom you recommended charged me $100.

    b) The doctor   you recommended charged me $100.

whom

What has been deleted from sentence **a** to form sentence **b**? ....

no

218. Can *who* in the sentence, *My aunt who lives in Chicago is very wealthy*, be deleted? ....

219. Compare the sentences of Frame 217 and 218 that were combined to form the complex sentences to determine when the substitute word can be deleted.

    a) *My aunt* is very wealthy.

    b) *My aunt* lives in Chicago.

    a) *The doctor* charged me $100.

    b) You recommended *the doctor*.

(direct) object

The substitute word can be deleted when the repeated NP is the .... of the embedded sentence.

220. Which of these sentences contain substitute words that can be deleted? (Indicate your answer by circling the substitute words that can be deleted.)

    a) The gun that John bought is broken.

    b) The gun that went off is broken.

    c) The lady who charged the fur coat is not my wife.

a) that   d) who

    d) The lady who I married did not buy a fur coat.

176

221. *That* can be used as a substitute for an NP that is not human as in the sentence, *The dog that bit me will be sorry*. Can *that* also substitute for repeated NP's that are human? Try it by combining these two sentences.

    a) The girl has bad breath.

    b) The girl kissed me.

c) The girl that kissed me has bad breath.

    c) ....

    ....

222. *That* can replace both human and nonhuman NP's. *Who* and *who(m)* are used only for human NP's. Can *which* be used to replace human NP's? Try it with these sentences.

    a) My cousin is from Holland.

    b) My cousin came to see me.

c) *My cousin which came to see me is from Holland* is unacceptable.

    c) ....

    ....

223. Put the substitute words *who*, *whom*, *which*, or *that* beside the appropriate statements (**a**, **b**, or **c**) below:

    a) Substitute for either human or nonhuman NP's:.........................

a) that

b) who, whom

c) which

    b) Substitute only for human NP's:..........................

    c) Substitute only for nonhuman NP's:.........................

224. We have been looking at one way in which simple sentences can be combined to form longer, more complex sentences. In the final section of this program, let's look at a rather complicated sentence and analyze it in terms of our rules for changing simple sentences into related and complex sentences. All the rules are processes that either add, delete, replace, or rearrange elements of basic sentences. What are the basic sentences that have been combined to form the sentence below? (Remember, basic sentences are those that have not undergone any of these processes.)

When will the doctor you called treat the child who was hit by a car?

a) The doctor will treat the child sometime.

b) you called the doctor

c) a car hit the child

    a) ....

    ....

    b) ....

    c) ....

225. Before these basic sentences could be combined, they had to undergo changes involving addition, deletion, replacement, and rearrangement. In basic sentence **a** (as given in the answer to the last frame), T + M has been rearranged, that is, moved, to the beginning of the sentence to produce the question:

....

....

Will the doctor treat the child sometime?

226. A replacement rule applied to sentence **a** substitutes .... for *sometime*, giving:

....

....

when
will the doctor treat the child when

227. A second rearrangement rule moves ....
to the beginning of the sentence, giving:

....

....

when

When will the doctor treat the child?

228. The second basic sentence (**b**) in Frame 224 is *you called the doctor*. Since sentence **b** repeats an NP of sentence **a**, we can .... the repeated NP, giving us:

....

replace

you called who(m)

229. By rearrangement, ... is moved to the beginning of the sentence, giving us:

....

who(m)

who(m) you called

230. Sentence **b** can now be embedded into sentence **a**, producing:

....

....

When will the doctor whom you recommended treat the child?

231. Since the substitute word *who(m)* replaced an NP that was the object in the embedded sentence, it may be ....

deleted

232. The third basic sentence (**c**) in Frame 224 is *a car hit the child*. This sentence contains a ....
verb; therefore it has a related ....
form, which is:

....

transitive
passive

The child was hit by a car.

178

233. Since sentence **c** repeats an NP of **b**, *the child* can be

replaced   who   .... by ....

234. We now have accounted for all the changes made in the three basic sentences, and have combined them to form the complex sentence of Frame 224. In addition to the process of embedding sentences into each other, the other processes that account for changes in basic sentences are:

a) the addition of elements   a) ....

b) the deletion of elements   b) ....

c) the replacement of elements   c) ....

d) the rearrangement of   d) ....
   elements

SUMMARY OF FRAMES 205–234

In this section, we have seen that rather complex sentences can be understood in terms of the combination of two or more basic sentences into one sentence. We also saw that before the basic sentences are combined, they may undergo a number of changes to form negatives, interrogatives, and passives.

To review the embedding of one sentence into another, let's look at these pairs of sentences:

a) The stranger ran away.   b) The stranger ran away.
   The stranger hit Tom.   Tom hit the stranger.

Both pairs of sentences include repeated Noun Phrases (*the stranger*). In the **a** pair, the repeated NP is the subject of the second sentence. In the **b** pair, the repeated NP is the object of the verb *hit*. If we wish to combine these sentences, we can replace the repeated NP with *who*, *whom*, or *that*. For the repeated NP that is the subject of the second sentence, our choice is either *who* or *that*. For the repeated NP that is an object, our choice is *who(m)* or *that*.

Making these substitutions for the repeated NP's we would have:

a) The stranger ran away.   b) The stranger ran away.

$\begin{Bmatrix} who \\ that \end{Bmatrix}$ hit Tom   Tom hit $\begin{Bmatrix} who \\ whom \\ that \end{Bmatrix}$

The second sentence of **a** can now be embedded into the first giving:

The stranger $\begin{Bmatrix} who \\ that \end{Bmatrix}$ hit Tom ran away.

However, before the second sentence of **b** can be embedded, we must switch the substitute word to the beginning of the sentence, giving:

$\begin{Bmatrix} who \\ whom \\ that \end{Bmatrix}$ Tom hit.

179

Finally, we can embed this sentence into the first sentence of **b**, giving:

$$\text{The stranger} \left\{ \begin{array}{l} \text{who} \\ \text{whom} \\ \text{that} \end{array} \right\} \text{Tom hit ran away.}$$

We also learned that the substitute word can optionally be deleted if it was a replacement for an NP that was the object of the embedded sentence. If we choose this option, our sentence will be:

The stranger Tom hit ran away.

It is not difficult to see that in a more extensive study other types of complicated English sentences could be understood by considering them as derivations of basic sentences that have undergone the processes of addition, deletion, replacement, and rearrangement.

Additional suggested readings in the study of English sentence grammar:

Jacobs, Roderick A., and Peter S. Rosenbaum, *English Transformational Grammar*, Waltham, Mass.: Blaisdell Publishing Company, 1968.

King, Harold B., *Guide and Workbook in the Structure of English*, Englewood Cliffs, N.J.: Prentice-Hall, Inc., 1966.

Thomas, Owen, *Transformational Grammar and the Teacher of English*, New York: Holt, Rinehart & Winston, Inc., 1965.